How to Study and Teach the Bible

How to Study and Teach the Bible

Julius R. Scruggs

TOWNSEND PRESS
Nashville, Tennessee

Copyright © 1994 by Townsend Press
All rights reserved.
Nashville, Tennessee
1-800-359-9398
Reprinted in 1995, 2000, 2003, 2005, 2015

No part of this book may be reproduced or transmitted in any form, by any means, electronic or mechanical, including photocopying, recording, or by any information storage or retrieval system without the expressed permission in writing from the publisher. Permission requests may be addresssed to Townsend Press, 330 Charlotte Avenue, Nashville, Tennessee 37201-1188; or e-mailed to customercare@sspbnbc.com.

Printed in the United States of America

Library of Congress Cataloging-in-Publication Data

Scruggs, Julius Richard.
   How to Study and Teach the Bible / by Julius R. Scruggs.
   p. cm.
   Includes bibliographical references.

   ISBN 0-910683-22-0
   1. Bible–Study and teaching. 2. Bible–Hermeneutics. I. Title
   BS600. 2. S35 1994   94-7845
   220' .07–dc20   CIP

Unless otherwise noted, Scripture quotations are from the King James Version. This publication utilizes Bible quotations from several translations. Widely used is the authorized King James Version, AD 1611. Periodically, some passages will be quoted from the New King James Version® of the Bible. Copyright © 1982 by Thomas Nelson. Used by permission. All rights reserved. Quotations from the Revised Standard Version of the Bible, Copyright 1946, 1952, 1971 and 1973 are used by permission from the National Council of Churches of Christ in the USA.

*Affectionately dedicated
to my wife, Josephine;
my daughter, Jennifer; my stepson, Marty;
and
to the First Baptist Church Family,
Huntsville, Alabama.*

Contents

Foreword ix

Acknowledgments xii

Introduction xiii

I   The Centrality of Bible Study in the Life
of the Church 1

II   What the Bible Is 10

III   Biblical Hermeneutics
(Guidelines for Interpreting the Bible) 28

IV   Tools and Aids for Bible Study and
Bible Teaching 46

V   How to Prepare a Bible Lesson 56

VI   The Students We Teach (Twos through Teens) 84

VII   The Teacher as Evangelist 97

Bibliography 106

Foreword

How to Study and Teach the Bible is a book whose time has come. Our times have never been riper for a manual which sets out, as its mission, to equip National Baptists with the wherewithal to know the Bible and utilize it in the battles of life. There has never been a time when the need for Christian education was more critical—the accumulation of knowledge of the Bible and the acquired ability for the dissemination of the same. This book opens up that possibility to the student who takes the time to inquire of its pages.

Julius Richard Scruggs is a well-trained scholar of the Bible, with a special fondness for the Old Testament. He is a long-standing National Baptist pastor with exceptional ability. He has pastored in three different states and now provides leadership for one of the strongest National Baptist congregations in the Alabama State Convention. He is a preacher par excellence. In addition, he is a superb teacher. All these attributes burst out upon you as you read his work in this publication. He carefully proceeds to provide equipment for the Bible student, teacher, preacher, or whoever desires to acquire armament for today's battle.

He begins by insisting that adequate time needs to be spent in the study of the Bible. So often, contemporary Christians devote so little time to study the Bible. In fact, some think such is simply unnecessary. He takes the position that the disciples of the early church accumulated a massive number of hours in firsthand study of God's Word at the feet of Jesus Christ, the Master Teacher. That being considered, he insists that the early disciples were better educated than someone who today holds a Ph.D. degree from a prominent university. His conclusion is that today's Christians must take seriously the example left to us by disciples of the early church. He wisely begins by addressing the composition of the Bible—what it really is. He carefully takes the reader through the Bible and its various strata of material, categories and kinds of books that compose the written form of the Word of God. Dr. Scruggs's treatment here is invaluable.

So often, Bible students are at a loss for direction as to how to dig out facts and information in and about the Bible. In the chapter, "Tools and Aids for Bible Study and Bible Teaching," the author sets before the reader the study tools that are indispensable to those who would dare to teach the Bible. The various versions of the Bible, Bible dictionaries, Bible concordances, Bible atlases, and the like are exposed to the Bible student and Sunday school teacher so they will know the resources that are available to enlarge their store of knowledge of the divine Word.

Dr. Scruggs enriches his work by sharing with the Bible student and Sunday school teacher an example of how a Bible lesson is prepared. This chapter speaks for itself. The author painstakingly lays out a model for teaching that even a neophyte in the Scripture can follow. After carefully studying this chapter, and surely after going over it a couple of times, a Bible student and/or Sunday school teacher will certainly emerge as a master at the craft.

The book ends with a significant study of the children we teach and how we can evangelize them through the church's Christian education programs. He discusses the various age levels of children as well as those things that make them peculiar at that age. He offers suggestions as to how to reach and teach children in respect to age group. Dr. Scruggs challenges the Sunday school teacher and anyone who engages in the teaching ministry in the church to make evangelism a central concern.

Julius Richard Scruggs is pastor of one of the finest National Baptist churches in the country—First Baptist Church of Huntsville, Alabama. Under his ministry, he has moved his congregation from a budget of less than $100,000 to nearly $1 million annually. His congregation is ministry oriented. Uniquely enough, Pastor Scruggs has grounded all of the ministries of his church in Christian education. Christian education thoroughly permeates every facet of church life at First Baptist.

It is indeed a pleasure to present this work by Dr. Scruggs. He and I have been personal friends for many years. We were born not far from one another in the same county in Tennessee—Giles. We matriculated at the same schools of higher education, American Baptist College and Vanderbilt Divinity School in Nashville, Tennessee. I personally know that his every word in this publication flows with passion and power: 1) passion for his people, the Negro people in the United States of America and the National Baptist Convention, USA, Inc., and the world. One would have to go far and look widely for someone who strives harder to make absolutely plain the understanding of the Word of God to His people; and 2) power, because his labor is under the unction and guidance of the Holy Spirit. With such passion and power, we offer this work to you, the pastor, Bible student, Sunday school teacher, and Christian educator alike. The Lord Jesus bless it for your good and to His glory.

Dr. Amos Jones Jr., Director
Christian Education Department
Sunday School Publishing Board, NBC, USA, Inc.
February 18, 1994

Acknowledgments

I am deeply grateful to Dr. Amos Jones Jr., former head of the Department of Christian Education at the Sunday School Publishing Board of the National Baptist Convention, USA, Inc., for asking me to write this study guide on *How to Study and Teach the Bible*.

I especially thank Mrs. Lillie W. Winston, my secretary, for the labor of love she gave in typing the manuscript for this book. Profound appreciation is expressed to the Reverend Earla Sue Lockhart for proofreading and offering invaluable editorial suggestions.

Profound thanks is also extended to the Reverend Michelle Cobb, who collaborated with me in writing chapter 6.

Finally, I owe a tremendous debt to my wife for her understanding and encouragement throughout this writing venture.

Introduction

The Bible is the most important book in the whole world. It is important because it deals with life and death, temporal and eternal issues, and with issues that impact every person's life at various levels. It is the most significant book because it contains the revelation of God in Jesus Christ, the highest revelation for the Christian that has ever been disclosed (Hebrews 1:1-3).

Therefore, the Bible should be carefully studied, taught, and applied by all persons everywhere. It is my belief that if all persons everywhere seriously internalize the message and Spirit of the Bible found in Jesus Christ, we would have a healthier and happier world. Our sense of responsibility and commitment to God and His world would be much wiser and more intense than it is presently.

Since I hold these strong convictions concerning the Bible, I therefore feel it befitting to write these chapters to facilitate teachers of the Bible in their study and teaching ministries.

Of course, this is not an exhaustive study by any means, but I do hope that you will find some value in these essays to aid in your ministries of teaching and proclamation.

Chapter I

The Centrality of Bible Study in the Life of the Church

It is the firm conviction of this author that Bible study in the Sunday school, midweek Bible classes, discipleship training groups, mission circles, and the like, is extremely important. In fact, there is no substitute for Bible study in the life of the Christian church. Either she lives and thrives by it or she dies without it. Consequently, every serious church body should develop and sustain a viable Bible teaching ministry, because without it, the church will be relegated to a ministry of mediocrity, and forced to be "a taillight for culture rather than being a headlight"—to borrow from Martin Luther King Jr.

The church must know that without a strong and systematic Bible teaching ministry, she will be "a pathetic echo rather than a prophetic voice"—to borrow a phrase from E. Stanley Jones. To say it another way, without a strong and systematic Bible teaching ministry, the church will be labeled as having a "Model-T Ford ministry" in a supersonic jet age. Dr. John Killinger, one of my major theological mentors, spoke to this issue when he wrote the following:

> Church attendees today are intelligent, eclectic, wary, increasingly independent, and restless—and no preacher is able to meet their needs more than partially in the Sunday morning sermon. How vastly important, then, has become the teaching ministry of the church, a ministry shared by competent and dedicated lay men and women who in effect form a variegated network of instruction, experimentation and counseling in support of the preaching and appropriation of the gospel.[1]

Why do I feel so strongly about a central, systematic, Bible teaching ministry in the church? First, because Christian theology has always firmly declared that God is all-wise. If God is all-wise, then should we ever take pleasure in being otherwise? If God is all-wise (and I firmly believe that He is), then we should want to be more like God. We should desire to be wise in the ways and will of God. And, we become wise in the ways and will of God primarily by personally knowing Him and by systematically studying His Word. In this technological and scientifically intelligent world, we need to know God as intimately and biblically as possible, so that we can be "wise as serpents and harmless as doves."

The second reason I believe strongly that a church should have a vital and systematic teaching ministry is because the Bible commands it. As far back as Deuteronomy, the Israelites were commanded to teach the law of God to their children on a systematic basis:

> "Now this is the commandment, and these are the statutes and judgments which the LORD your God has commanded to teach you, that you may observe them in the land which you are crossing over to possess,
>
> "that you may fear the LORD your God, to keep all His statutes and His commandments which I command you, you and your son and your grandson, all the days of your life, and that your days may be prolonged.
>
> "Therefore hear, O Israel, and be careful to observe it, that it may be well with you, and that you may multiply greatly as the LORD God of your fathers has promised you—'a land flowing with milk and honey.'
>
> "Hear, O Israel: The LORD our God, the LORD is one!
>
> "You shall love the LORD your God with all your heart, with all your soul, and with all your strength.
>
> "And these words which I command you today shall be in your heart.

"You shall teach them diligently to your children, and shall talk of them when you sit in your house, when you walk by the way, when you lie down, and when you rise up.

"You shall bind them as a sign on your hand, and they shall be as frontlets between your eyes.

"You shall write them on the doorposts of your house and on your gates." (Deuteronomy 6:1-9, NKJV)

If that was a requirement for people under the Old Covenant, how much more is it necessary for us who are under the New Covenant to teach systematically the Word of God to our children today? Many of the crises which our culture faces—crises of drug and alcohol abuse, crises of mounting teenage pregnancies, crises of the AIDS epidemic, crises of racism and sexism, crises of hunger and poverty, war and the like—all find footage in our neglect to teach seriously and systematically the Word of God in our homes and churches.

I am often intrigued by our modern cry that Madalyn Murray O'Hair, through federal legislation, caused us not to be able to have prayer in our schools. While I understand what persons are seeking to say in this instance, I am reminded that Mrs. O'Hair did not really and truly cause Christians to lose prayer and meditation in public places. Before prayer was removed from the schools, we had already (many of us) allowed it to die in the home(s). We need to rethink Deuteronomy 6 and teach our children—at home and at church—the Word of God. If they get solid biblical training at home and at church, then when they get to school they will know how to pray, regardless of legal restrictions. Nobody can stop a dedicated Christian teacher from praying at school. Nobody can stop a dedicated Christian student from praying at school. There is plenty of time at school to whisper a prayer to God and allow that prayer to direct your conduct.

More importantly, Jesus, the Master Teacher, mandated that the church should be serious about its teaching ministry. The book of Matthew, perhaps, emphasizes this as well as any of the other

Gospels. Matthew pictures Jesus as the teacher par excellence: "And seeing the multitudes, he went up into a mountain: and when he was set [the Rabbis normally taught by remaining seated], his disciples came unto him: And he opened his mouth and TAUGHT them..." (Matthew 5:1-2, KJV, emphasis added). Let us further elaborate on the seriousness of Jesus' teaching ministry with His disciples, especially the Twelve. Jesus was so serious about teaching His twelve disciples that He spent three (3) years teaching them the will and message of God. Some people believe that Jesus' disciples were ignorant and unlearned. These misguided people have taken their clues from what some misguided Sadducees and Pharisees said about Jesus' disciples. Acts 4:13a states what these Sadducees and Pharisees said:

> "Now when they saw the boldness of Peter and John, and perceived that they were unlearned and ignorant men, they marvelled...."

I would remind us, however, that Jesus' disciples were neither ignorant nor unlearned. In fact, they had more than our modern day equivalent of a Ph.D. degree in religion and theology. Let me illustrate this point. Compare our modern theological education requirements with the disciples' training as they studied with Jesus, the Master Teacher. First, they had the best teacher. Nobody equals Jesus when it comes to teaching the Word and will of God. He is indeed the Master Teacher.

I was blessed to have some great teachers in college and seminary, but none of them can be compared with Jesus. Their wisdom could not and cannot match Jesus' wisdom. Not only did Jesus' disciples have the best teacher, but they also put in more hours in their educational studies than people who earn their Ph.D. in religion and theology in our best schools. For example, a person who has an earned doctor of philosophy degree in religion attends college for four years, which means a person spends about 140 semester hours to earn a college degree. Then the person enrolls in seminary for three years and spends about 90 semester hours to earn a master of divinity degree. Next, the person spends around 90 more semester hours to earn a Ph.D. degree in religion or theology. Let us compute the person's hours:

    140 hours Bachelor degree
      90 hours Master of Divinity degree
      90 hours Doctor of Philosophy degree
    320 Total hours

Thus, you see that a person with an earned Ph.D. in religion has put in about 320 semester hours. And that person is now considered an expert in the field. That person is truly educated. Now let us observe the twelve disciples' training with Jesus and compare. The Twelve studied with Jesus for about three years, sometimes day and night. But let us be conservative and let us not count their night classes. Let us not even count the days when they spent twelve to fourteen hours with Jesus. Let us simply give them credit for eight (8)-hour days of study. Since they were with Him in school three hundred and sixty-five days per year, let's multiply 365 times eight hours:

    365 days
       8 hours per day
  2,920 hours

You remember that they spent almost three years as His students. Consequently, one must now multiply 2,920 hours by three (3) years:

  2,920 hours
      3 years
  8,760 hours

Thus, you can see that the disciples of Jesus spent about 8,760 hours with the Master Teacher, while those pursuing the Ph.D. in religion and theology today only spend 320 semester hours with our teachers. Tell me, then, who is unlearned and ignorant—the disciples or us? It is obvious that the disciples were learned men because they had spent many hours with Jesus, the Master Teacher. So, we can see that Jesus was very serious about the teaching and "Bible Study" ministry of the church. For Jesus, teaching and the Word and will of God was of utmost importance. Should it not be the same with us?

Additionally, the early church was serious about the centrality of the teaching ministry. In fact, the New Testament church took its cue from Jesus. Two passages of Scripture come to mind: first, Matthew 28:19-20; and second, Acts 2:41-42. In both these passages, the church took Jesus' teaching ministry seriously and implemented it systematically. In the Matthean passage, they remembered that Jesus said, "Go therefore and make disciples of all nations,... teaching them to observe all things whatever I have commanded you...."; and over in the Acts passage, they implemented what Jesus mandated. Acts 2:41-42 states, "Then those who gladly received his word were baptized; and that day about three thousand souls were added to them. And THEY continued steadfastly in the apostles' doctrine [teaching] and fellowship, in the breaking of bread, and in prayers" (NKJV, emphasis added). These two verses highlight the seriousness with which the apostles of Jesus took their teaching ministries. You recall that these three thousand souls (persons) who were converted to Christianity on the Day of Pentecost were babes in Christian doctrine. Therefore, the apostles taught these three thousand persons, continuously and systematically, the doctrines of the church—doctrines that Jesus had already taught them (the apostles) during His earthly ministry.

What doctrines do you suppose the text has in mind? ("And they continued steadfastly in the apostles' doctrines....") I contend they were talking about all the doctrines that Jesus had taught them. For example, they studied the doctrine of the kingdom of God, which was an umbrella doctrine for Jesus. They studied the following doctrines:

- God
  a. God the Father
  b. God the Son
- God's Purpose of Grace
- The Church
- Baptism

- c. God the Holy Spirit
- Word of God (the Bible)
- Man (humanity)
- Salvation
  - a. Regeneration
    - 1) Repentance
    - 2) Faith
    - 3) Justification
  - b. Sanctification
  - c. Glorification
- The Lord's Supper
- The Lord's Day
- The Last Thing (Eschatology)
- Missions and Evangelism
- Stewardship
- The Fruit of the Spirit
- The Gifts of the Spirit
- And others

Thus, you can see that each new convert in the early church was taught the doctrines of the church. They were educated in the "milk" as well as the "meat" of the faith. If we are going to have strong and effective churches, we, too, must be serious about teaching all that the Lord has commanded us to teach. We must be serious about teaching the "apostles' doctrines." Every member of the church should not only have an intimate experience with the Lord—an experience which the Bible calls "born again," "conversion," "saved," "committed to the Lord," etc.—but every member must also be serious about the doctrines of the Lord. We must know them spiritually and intellectually and live them pragmatically. And, especially, all pastors and teachers in the church's Christian Education Department should know the doctrines of the Lord—the theology of the church. Howard P. Colson highlights this point when he quotes Findley B. Edge:

> On the basis of his understanding of the Bible and the Christian faith, the teacher inevitably teaches theology. It is highly important, regardless of the age group being taught that the teacher be aware of the theology he is teaching and that it has been arrived at on the basis of a careful, intelligent study of the teachings of the Scriptures. What doctrine of God is being taught to the child in the nursery department? Or what view of the church is being taught? One three-year-old child was greatly confused because the teacher referred to the church building as "God's house,"

but the child complained, "I never see God in His house." What view of prayer is being taught to the child in the beginner's department?

Some small children have had their faith in prayer greatly shaken because when they prayed for their grandmother to get well, God didn't "answer" their prayer. What view of Jesus is taught to the nursery, beginner, and primary children? What view of sin and salvation is being taught to the junior boy or girl? We often seek to lead the children into a personal encounter with Jesus in a conversion experience and to a commitment of their lives to Him. How adequately do we help them to understand the meaning of this experience and to understand what is involved in it? What kind of theology do we teach the intermediates and young people? Is it a theology that is both so intelligent and firmly rooted that when they come face-to-face with conflicting points of view—perhaps in college—they will not be swept off their feet because they have considered these conflicting points of view previously in the Sunday school under the guidance of a Christian teacher?[2]

There is no excuse for church leaders' not knowing and teaching the doctrines of the church—the Word of God.

Acts 2:42 not only encourages the church's pastors and teachers to be serious about teaching the doctrines of our Lord, but it also mandates that they be serious about understanding and developing the warmth of fellowship in every local congregation. The thick chunks of doctrine may be too difficult at points for the children, but when they cannot intellectually grasp heavy theology, they can understand a friendly, Christian smile or handshake. Teaching doctrine and participating in the warm fellowship of believers are extremely significant. For, fellowship is to the Christian what water is to the fish. It is his home. It is where he finds his "daily bread." Our culture is starving for the Bread of Life—the written and "living Word" of God.

Someone may ask, how do we develop and maintain a strong, Bible-teaching ministry in the church? First, the pastors must be serious about and committed to this ministry. If pastors are not serious and committed, the teaching ministry can live, but not with the power and momentum that it could have if they had provided serious leadership. Furthermore, if pastors are serious Bible students, they must know that not only did the apostles in Acts 2:42 give strong leadership in the church's teaching ministry, but also that Paul listed one of the gifts of the Spirit as pastor and teacher (Ephesians 4:11-12). Here, Paul clearly states that the pastor or pastor/teacher is an equipper of the saints (the members) for the work of the ministry. Thus, every pastor/teacher is an enabler and a facilitator in the teaching ministry of the church. That does not mean that a pastor has to teach a class. But it does mean that pastors must teach and equip others in order to facilitate the ministry of the church and to help teachers handle classes and departments on their own. In many larger churches today, the pastor has a salaried minister or director of Christian education who takes the greater responsibility for teaching Christian lay persons how to teach the Word of God. In smaller churches, the teaching and equipping role is done primarily by the pastor. Whether the pastor does it, the director of Christian education, or both, the job must be done. The church (especially lay persons) must be equipped to teach the Word of God, a word that must be

- biblically based.
- doctrinally sound.
- life-centered.

NOTES

1. John Killinger, *The Centrality of Preaching in the Total Task of the Ministry* (Waco, Texas: Word Books, 1969), 73.

2. Howard P. Colson, *Preparing to Teach the Bible* (Nashville, Tennessee: Convention Press, 1959), 5.

Chapter II

What the Bible Is

Many scholars have rightly asserted that the Bible is a library of books, not just one single book. In fact, there are sixty-six books in the Bible—thirty-nine in the Old Testament and twenty-seven in the New Testament. The word *Bible* itself comes from two Greek words: *biblion*, meaning "book," and *biblio*, meaning "little books." Thus the Bible is a collection of sixty-six little books written by many authors over a long period of time.

In this chapter, we are particularly concerned with the general composition and content of the Bible. In this light, every Bible student is aware that there are two main divisions of our Christian Bible: the Old and New Testaments or the Old and New Covenants.

Structure and Composition

The Old Testament, first and foremost, the Bible of the Jews, is composed of three divisions of literature, which is arranged differently from our English Bible. The divisional structure of the Hebrew (Jewish) Bible is composed of

(1) **The Law** (Torah) also called **Pentateuch**

    Genesis   Numbers
    Exodus   Deuteronomy
    Leviticus

(2) **The Prophets**

    a. *The Former Prophets*
    Joshua   1 and 2 Samuel
    Judges   1 and 2 Kings

b. *The Latter Prophets*

Isaiah	Micah
Jeremiah	Nahum
Ezekiel	Habakkuk
Hosea	Zephaniah
Joel	Haggai
Amos	Zechariah
Obadiah	Malachi
Jonah	

(3) **The Writings** (Hagiographa)

Psalms	Ecclesiastes
Proverbs	Esther
Job	Daniel
Song of Solomon	Ezra
or Song of Songs	Nehemiah
Ruth	1 and 2 Chronicles
Lamentations	

In comparison, our English Bible has the following structural composition:

(1) **The Law** (Pentateuch)

Genesis	Numbers
Exodus	Deuteronomy
Leviticus	

(2) **Books of History**

Joshua	1 and 2 Chronicles
Judges	Ezra
Ruth	Nehemiah
1 and 2 Samuel	Esther
1 and 2 Kings	

(3) **The Books of Wisdom Literature** (Poetry)

Job	Ecclesiastes
Psalms	Song of Solomon
Proverbs	

(4) **The Prophets** (Major and Minor)

Isaiah	Jonah
Jeremiah	Micah
Lamentations	Nahum
Ezekiel	Habakkuk
Daniel	Zephaniah
Hosea	Haggai
Joel	Zechariah
Amos	Malachi
Obadiah	

It may be noted that the Law is the same in the Hebrew and English Bibles. But there is a significant difference in book arrangements in the other divisions. For example, the Hebrew Bible lists Ezra, Nehemiah, Daniel, Lamentations, Esther, 1 and 2 Chronicles, Job, Song of Solomon, Psalms, Proverbs, and Ruth among "The Writings." In our English Bible, however, Daniel and Lamentations are listed among the Minor Prophets. Psalms, Job, Proverbs, Song of Solomon, and Ecclesiastes are listed among the *Books of Poetry* or *Wisdom Literature*. Ruth, Ezra, Nehemiah, and 1 and 2 Chronicles are listed among the books of history.

Please note also that the books of Joshua through 2 Kings are listed in the Hebrew Bible as "Former Prophets." Because prophets may have written these books, they are designated as "Former Prophets."

The Old Testament Apocrypha

Have you ever thumbed through a Bible and come across some unfamiliar books? A friend told me of an incident that occurred when he was called upon to read the Sunday morning Scripture lesson. He said that he proceeded to the pulpit, opened the big Bible, and began looking for the book of Habakkuk. Unfortunately, when he opened the Bible, he began seeing books like Tobit and 1 and 2 Esdras. He had come upon books that we call apocryphal. These books are in the Catholic Bibles and currently in some Protestant Bibles, especially the *New Oxford Annotated Bibl*e with the

Apocrypha. The apocryphal books were present in the Greek version of the Old Testament used in Alexandria, Egypt, and other cities of the Roman world at the time of the rise of Christianity, but were not included in the Hebrew Old Testament. When Jerome translated the Catholic Bible, known as the Latin Vulgate, he included these apocryphal books. They have remained in the Catholic Bible to this day. Protestants, however, do not believe these books have been divinely inspired; therefore, we do not use them as authoritative Scripture. But it is wise to know about them, especially to the extent that we are not embarrassed, as my friend was when he found them in the pulpit Bible and did not know what they were or from whence they came. For informational purposes, the Old Testament apocryphal books are

1 Esdras
2 Esdras
Tobit
Judith
Additions to Esther
The Wisdom of Solomon
Ecclesiasticus, or the Wisdom of Jesus the Son of Sirach
Baruch
The Letter of Jeremiah
The Prayer of Azariah and the Song of the Three Young Men
Susanna
Bel and the Dragon
The Prayer of Manasseh
1 Maccabees
2 Maccabees

The New Testament

The New Testament is composed of (1) four Gospels: Matthew, Mark, Luke, and John, which give four portraits of the life and teachings of Jesus; (2) the book of Acts, which mirrors the words and deeds of the New Testament church as it was directed to spread the Gospel by the power of the Holy Spirit; (3) twenty-one letters written by inspired persons to churches of that day addressing particular needs which arose in those times with application for both then and now; and (4) an apocalypse (book of Revelation), which reveals that Christ and His church will be victorious in spite of persecution, suffering, death, opposition, and all evil forces.

The Essential Message and Character of the Bible

Now that we have focused on the composition and structure of the Bible, we move on to look at its essential message and character. Why were sixty-six books written? What central message(s) do they contain? What do these messages mean for modern persons living in diverse places and cultures in the world?

(1) **The Essential Content of the Bible**

The Bible is a human-divine book, inspired by the Holy Spirit, and sent through human personalities as they recorded God's revelation for then and for now.

Note carefully our suggestion that the Bible is God's revelation (self-disclosure) of Himself to people. This is true from Genesis to Revelation. After God had revealed to the writer of the book of Genesis the divine creation of the whole world, including mankind, He quickly moved on to show how He revealed Himself to one man, Abraham, and called that man to be a bearer of a universal covenant message. This revelation of God to Abraham is contained in chapter 12 of the book of Genesis:

> Now the LORD said to Abram, "Go from your country and your kindred and your father's house to the land that I will show you. And I will make of you a great nation, and I will bless you, and make your name great, so that you will be a blessing. I will bless those who bless you, and him who curses you I will curse; and by you all the families of the earth shall bless themselves." (Genesis 12:1-3, RSV)

These verses disclose the beginning of God's revelation to the Hebrew people, the covenant people of the Old Testament. It is of particular importance that God's grace is at work in His revelation of Himself to Abraham. His revelation and call to Abraham are solely of grace because Abraham had not done anything to earn, merit, or deserve this gracious act on God's part. He was called to be the father of a covenant people simply because of God's goodness. God desired to bless His world, and chose Abraham as a channel or vessel through which these divine blessings would flow.

This fact is true throughout the Bible and becomes the essential theological current of the entire Bible. That is, all the blessings that have come to humankind have been initiated by the grace of God. When we look later at the character and content of the New Testament, we will see even clearer that God, who revealed Himself to humankind in Jesus the Christ, was full of grace.

The God who reveals Himself graciously to people also needs persons to respond to His graceful offers. And so, Abraham responded positively to God's call. He obeyed God. That is why he stands out as the spiritual giant of the Old Testament. Without a Bible or any written Word of God, this man heard God speaking to him in the inner chambers of his spirit and obeyed His voice, call, and commission. If people are to be really blessed today, they must have a religion like Abraham—a faith that results in obedience to God's will for their lives.

It is also of extreme importance that God told Abraham that through him all the families of the Earth would be blessed (Genesis 12:3b). All the families of the Earth included not only the Hebrew people, but also the Gentile people then and now. Thus, from the very beginning, God's love was extended to all races, ethnic groups, and peoples of the universe. This same vision of God's wide love and mercy for all mankind is highlighted again in the book of Isaiah:

> "It is too light a thing that you should be my servant to raise up
> the tribes of Jacob and to restore the preserved of Israel; I will

give you as a light to the nations, that my salvation may reach to the end of the earth. (Isaiah 49:6, RSV)

This text struck Norman K. Gottwald with such tremendous power and impact that he named his book about the Old Testament *A Light to the Nations*. And so, even in the Old Testament, God's revelation of Himself from the beginning was a gracious and loving revelation. The Bible teacher must always keep this in mind when teaching and expounding the Word of God.

As one reads the Bible book by book from Genesis to Revelation, the theme of God's calling people to be bearers and heralds of His covenant grace is clearly seen. It is true in Joshua, Judges, Ruth, 1 and 2 Samuel, 1 and 2 Kings, and it is especially true in the prophetic books. We are informed that the prophets were called of God to go and speak for Him the Word of God.

In many places in prophetic literature, we find the phrase "Thus saith the Lord," meaning that the prophets were not speaking their own words, but were indeed sharing the words of God. *And so, the essential character of the Bible is that it is the revealed Word of God for then and for now*. Thus, when teachers teach and preachers preach and people witness from the Bible, we are sharing the Word of God and not our own word. Therefore, it is extremely important that we pray and study that we may "rightly divide" the revealed Word of God (the Word of Truth).

(2) **Progressive Revelation**

In 1962, the authors of the little pamphlet "The Baptist Faith and Message" revised and updated "The New Hampshire Confession of Faith"—a statement of faith by which all Baptists have been governed from its inception. In the first article or statement of faith, the authors addressed the issue of Scripture.

THE SCRIPTURE

The Holy Bible was written by men divinely inspired and is the record of God's revelation of Himself to man. It is a perfect treasure of divine instruction.

It has God for its author, salvation for its end, and truth, without any mixture of error, for its matter. It reveals the principles by which God judges us; and therefore is, and will remain to the end of the world, the true center of Christian union and the supreme standard by which all human conduct, creeds, and religious opinions should be tried. The criterion by which the Bible is to be interpreted is Jesus Christ.

This statement of faith focuses on much that we have already noted in this discourse. However, toward the end, there is a statement that must claim our attention at this point in our discussion. The statement is this:

"The criterion by which the Bible is to be interpreted is Jesus Christ."

This statement demands that we deal with the idea of progressive revelation. We have already seen that God revealed Himself to Abraham in purposeful and graceful ways. Likewise, He revealed Himself to Moses in purposeful and graceful ways. Perhaps the highest revelation that He gave to Moses was on the mountain of Sinai where he received the Ten Commandments, a lofty and holy set of laws. Moreover, He revealed His covenant and ethical will to the prophets, especially the eighth-century Prophets—Isaiah, Hosea, Amos, and Micah.

Who could miss the lofty ethical and covenant demands of God in Amos 5:21-24?

"I hate, I despise your feasts, and I take no delight in your solemn assemblies. Even though you offer me your burnt offerings and cereal offerings, I will not accept them, and the peace offerings of your fatted beasts I will not look upon. Take away from me the noise of your songs; to the melody of your harps I will not listen. But let justice roll down like waters, and righteousness like an everflowing stream." (RSV)

Who could overlook the holy vision of God to Isaiah in chapter 6:1-8? Or who could miss Isaiah's message from God that Israel was to be a light to the nations? (Isaiah 49:6). Or who could not understand the profound message with New Testament implications of the "suffering servant" passage in Isaiah 53:3-6?

> He was despised and rejected by men; a man of sorrows, and acquainted with grief; and as one from whom men hide their faces he was despised, and we esteemed him not. Surely he has borne our griefs and carried our sorrows; yet we esteemed him sticken, smitten by God, and afflicted. But he was wounded for our transgressions, he was bruised for our iniquities; upon him was the chastisement that made us whole, and with his stripes we are healed. All we like sheep have gone astray; we have turned every one to his own way; and the LORD has laid on him the iniquity of us all. (RSV)

Who could not discern the deep and unconditional love of God revealed in Hosea 11:1-4, 8-9?

> When Israel was a child, I loved him, and out of Egypt I called my son. The more I called them, the more they went from me; they kept sacrificing to the Baals, and burning incense to idols. Yet it was I was who taught Ephraim to walk, I took them up in my arms; but they did not know that I healed them. I led them with cords of compassion, with the bands of love, and I became to them as one who eases the yoke on their jaws, and I bent down to them and fed them. . . . How can I give you up, O Ephraim! How can I hand you over, O Israel! How can I make you like Admah! How can I treat you like Zeboiim! My heart recoils within me, my compassion grows warm and tender. I will not execute my fierce anger, I will not again destroy Ephraim; for I am God and not man, the Holy One in your midst, and I will not come to destroy. (RSV)

Who could miss the remarkable and immortal covenant trilogy in Micah 6:8?

> He has shown you, O man, what is good; And what does the LORD require of you But to do justly, To love mercy, And to walk humbly with your God? (NKJV)

Then there are Jeremiah and others who spoke prophetically the will of God at later periods in Israel's covenant history. Even when Israel had sinned and violated her covenant relationship with God, the Lord punished her, but He was still faithful to His gracious covenant promise. Listen to Jeremiah as he shared with the people in Babylonian exile:

> "For thus says the LORD: When seventy years are completed for Babylon, I will visit you, and I will fulfil to you my promise and bring you back to this place. For I know the plans I have for you, says the LORD, plans for welfare and not for evil, to give you a future and a hope. (Jeremiah 29:10-11, RSV)

And again, listen to Jeremiah share God's Word concerning Israel, God's covenant people—a word for her future.

> Thus says the LORD: "The people who survived the sword found grace in the wilderness; when Israel sought for rest, the LORD appeared to him from afar. I have loved you with an everlasting love; therefore I have continued my faithfulness to you.". . ."Behold, the days are coming, says the LORD, when I will make a new covenant with the house of Israel and the house of Judah, not like the covenant which I made with their fathers when I took them by the hand to bring them out of the land of Egypt, my covenant which they broke, though I was their husband, says the LORD. But this is the covenant which I will make with the house of Israel after those days, says the LORD: I will put my law within them, and I will write it upon their hearts; and I will be their God, and they shall be my people. And no longer shall each man teach his neighbor and each his brother, saying,'Know the LORD,' for they shall all know me, from the

least of them to the greatest, says the LORD; for I will forgive their iniquity, and I will remember their sin no more." (Jeremiah 31:2-3, 31-34, RSV)

Any serious student of the Bible can see the high and holy will of God in these passages. But what about other passages in the Old Testament where the expression of the will of God does not seem to measure up to the lofty understandings of His revealed will in Christ? What about passages like "an eye for an eye and tooth for a tooth"? (Exodus 21:24). What about the law in Leviticus that the child who curses his father or mother shall be put to death? "For every one who curses his father or his mother shall be put to death; he has cursed his father or his mother, his blood is upon him" (Leviticus 20:9, RSV). What about the law of adultery which stated that those who were caught in adultery were to be put to death, both male and female? ("If a man commits adultery with the wife of his neighbor, both the adulterer and adulteress shall be put to death" [Leviticus 20:10, RSV].) What about the idea of killing everyone in the holy war, even women, children, and cattle? "Thus says the LORD of hosts, I will punish what Amalek did to Israel in opposing them on the way, when they came up out of Egypt. Now go and smite Amalek, and utterly destroy all that they have; do not spare them, but kill both man and woman, infant and suckling, ox and sheep, camel and ass'" (1 Samuel 15:2-3, RSV).

The serious student of biblical ethics has a problem dealing with these passages as they are. Suppose today in a given church of two thousand members, we are told to kill every child who has cursed his parents; kill every person who has committed adultery or fornication; go forth to war and kill everybody including women, innocent babies, children, animals, everything; suppose you applied the principle of an eye for an eye and a tooth for a tooth! What do you think would be the result in this church of two thousand? Many people would die; many others would suffer unnecessarily, all because we have not allowed the ethical standards of the Old Covenant (Old Testament) to be updated to the New Covenant (New Testament).

Now, then, that is why that last statement was included in the article of faith on "The Scriptures." The criterion (standard or measurement) by which the Bible is to be interpreted is Jesus Christ. All Scripture, therefore, must be measured by Jesus' standard before it can become the final and perfect revelation of God (see chapter 3). Jesus, in dealing with the woman caught in adultery (John 8), would not allow the men to apply the law of the Old Covenant, but extended the mercy and grace of God to the woman caught in adultery. In short, "He looked beyond her fault and saw her need," to use a line from a modern gospel song. He saved her. He did not allow them to murder her. Today, Jesus would not be pleased with a child being put to death for cursing his parents. The child who does this ugly act certainly should be punished, but not put to death as the Old Testament demands.

Today, Jesus would not send a nation to war to kill innocent children and babies or cattle and other animals. In fact, as stated in an earlier chapter, Jesus demands that we love our enemies (Matthew 5:44), and pray for those who misuse and abuse us. Jesus' understanding of the revelation and will of God is the highest and most perfect that has ever been given. *Therefore, the doctrine of progressive revelation demands that we view all Scripture through the mind and eye of Jesus.* All Scripture must be measured by His words and deeds, in order for it to meet and fulfill the perfect will of God! Every teacher and preacher must clearly understand this fact if he is to correctly teach and proclaim the Word of God (see Hebrews 1:1-2).

(3) The Bible and Comprehensive Needs

As we reflect on what the Bible is, it is necessary to point out that for the Christian, the Bible addresses our comprehensive needs. As we face problems, challenges, opportunities, frustrations, fears, injustices, racism, sexism, classism, doubts, aspirations, and the like, the Bible addresses these and many more. Here is an informative section from the back of a copy of the *New King James Version* of the Bible entitled, "Finding Help in the Bible."

FINDING HELP IN THE BIBLE
Help in Special Circumstances

Being a friend
Proverbs 17:17;
Luke 10:25-37;
John 15:11-17;
Romans 16:1-2

Being a leader
Isaiah 11:1-9;
Isaiah 32:1-8
1 Timothy 3:1-7; 2:14-26;
2 Timothy 2:14-26;
Titus 1:5-9

Caring for the aged and widowed
Genesis 47:1-12;
Ruth 1;
Proverbs 23:22;
1 Timothy 5:3-8

Celebrating a marriage
Genesis 2:18-24;
Song of Songs 8:6-7;
Ephesians 4:21-33;
Colossians 2:6-7

Celebrating a wedding anniversary
Psalm 100;
1 Corinthians 13

Celebrating birth/adoption of a child
Psalm 100;
Proverbs 22:6;
Luke 18:15-17;
John 16:16-22

Celebrating a graduation
Psalm 119:105-106;
Proverbs 9:10-12;

Galatians 5:16-26;
Philippians 4:4-9

Controlling your temper
Proverbs 14:17, 29; 15:18;
19:11; 29:22;
Ecclesiastes 7:9;
Galatians 5:16-26

Controlling your tongue
Psalms 12; 19:14;
Proverbs 11:13; 26:20;
2 Thessalonians 2:16-17
James 3:1-12

Discovering God's will
Psalm 15;
Micah 6:6-8;
Matthew 5:1-14;
Luke 9:21-27;
Romans 13:8-14;
2 Peter 1:3-9;
1 John 4:7-21

Encountering a cult
Matthew 7:15-20;
2 Peter 2;
1 John 4:1-6;
Jude

Encountering peer pressure
Proverbs 1:7-19;
Romans 12:1-2;
Galatians 6:1-5;
Ephesians 5:1-20

Entering college
Proverbs 2:1-8;

Proverbs 3:1-18;
Proverbs 4:1-27;
Proverbs 23:12;
Romans 8:1-17;
1 Corinthians 1:18-31

Entering military service
2 Samuel 22:2-51;
Psalm 91;
Ephesians 6:10-20;
2 Timothy 2:13

Experiencing a loved one's death
Job 19:25-27;
John 11:25-27;
John 14:1-7;
Romans 8:31; 14:7-9
1 Thessalonians 4:13-18

Experiencing illness
Psalm 23;
Mark 1:29-34;
Mark 6:53-56;
James 5:14-16

Experiencing suffering and persecution
Psalm 109;
Psalm 119:153-160;
Matthew 5:3-12;
John 15:18; 16:4;
Romans 8:18-30;
2 Corinthians 4:1-15;
Hebrews 12:1-11;
1 Peter 4:12-19

Facing a difficult decision
1 Kings 3;
Esther 4:7;
Psalm 139;
Daniel 2:14-23;
Colossians 3:12-17

Facing a divorce
Psalm 25;
Matthew 19:3-9;
Philippians 3:1-11

Facing a natural disaster
Genesis 8:1-9, 17;
Job 36:22; 37:13;
Psalms 29:124; 36:5-9;
Jeremiah 31:35-37;
Romans 8:31-39;
1 Peter 1:1-3

Facing a trial or lawsuit
Psalm 26;
Isaiah 50:4-11;
Matthew 5:25-26;
Luke 18:1-8

Facing homelessness
Psalm 90:1-2;
Isaiah 65:17-25;
Lamentations 3:19-24;
Luke 9:57-62;
Revelation 21:1-4

Facing imprisonment
Lamentations 3:34-36;
Matthew 25:31-46;
Luke 4:16-21

Facing life alone
1 Corinthians 7:25-38; 12:1-31

Losing your job
Jeremiah 29:10-14;
Luke 16:1-13;
Philippians 4:10-13

Losing your property and possessions
Job 1:13-22;
Job 2:1-17;
Isaiah 30:19-26; 41:17-20;
Romans 8:18-39

Managing your time
Proverbs 12:11; 28:19;
Mark 13:32-37;
Luke 21:34-36;
1 Timothy 4:11-16;
Titus 3:8-14

Moving into a new home
Psalm 127:1-2;
Proverbs 24:3-4;
John 14:1-7;
Ephesians 3:14-21;
Revelation 3:20-21

Overcoming a grudge
Leviticus 19:17-18;
Matthew 5:23-26;
Luke 6:27-36;
Ephesians 4:25-32

Overcoming addiction
Psalms 40:1-5, 11-17; 116:1-7;
Proverbs 23:29-35;
2 Corinthians 5:16-21;
Ephesians 4:22-24

Overcoming prejudice
Matthew 7:1-5;
Acts 10:34-36;
Galatians 3:26-29;
Ephesians 2:11-22;
Colossians 3:5-11;
James 2:1-13

Overcoming pride
Psalm 131;
Mark 9:33-37;
Luke 14:7-11;
Luke 18:9-14;
1 Corinthians 1:18-31;
2 Corinthians 12:1-10

Overcoming procrastination
Matthew 22:1-14; 25:1-13;
2 Corinthians 6:1-2

Raising children
Proverbs 22:6;
Ephesians 6:4;
Colossians 3:21

Respecting civil authorities
Mark 12:13-17;
Romans 13:1-7;
Titus 3:1-2;
1 Peter 2:13-17

Respecting parents
Exodus 20:12;
Proverbs 23:22;
Ephesians 6:1-3;
Colossians 3:20

Retiring from your job
Numbers 6:24-26;
Psalm 145;
Matthew 25:31-46;
Romans 12:1-2;
Philippians 3:12-21;
2 Peter 1:2

Seeking forgiveness
Psalms 32:1-5; 51;
Proverbs 28:13;
Joel 2:12-17;
Matthew 6:14-15;
Luke 15;
Philemon;
Hebrews 4:14-16;
John 1:5-10

Seeking God's help
Psalms 5:57; 86; 121; 130;
Psalm 119:169-176;
Matthew 7:7-12

Seeking justice
Psalms 10:17; 75; 94;
Isaiah 42:1-7; 61:1-9;
Amos 5:21-24;
Habakkuk 1:1-2, 4

Seeking salvation
John 3:1-21;
Romans 1:16-17; 3:21-31; 5:1-11; 10:5-13;
Ephesians 1:3-14; 2:1-10

Seeking strength
Psalms 46; 138;
Isaiah 40:27-31; 51:12-16;

Ephesians 6:10-20;
2 Thessalonians 2:16-17

Seeking truth
Psalm 119:153-160;
John 8:31-47; 14:6-14;
16:4b-15;
1 Timothy 2:1-7

Sharing your gifts
Exodus 35:20-29;
Malachi 3:6-12;
Luke 21:1-4;
Acts 2:43-47;
Acts 4:32-37;
Romans 12:9-13;
2 Corinthians 9:6-15

Starting a new job
Proverbs 11:3;
Proverbs 22:29;
Romans 12:3-11;
1 Thessalonians 5:12-18;
2 Thessalonians 3:6-13;
1 Peter 4:7-11

Understanding your relationship with God
Deuteronomy 5:1-22;
Psalm 139;
John 15:1-17;
Romans 5:1-11; 8:1-17

Understanding your relationship with others
Deuteronomy 5:16-21;
Proverbs 3:27-35;
Matthew 18:15-17; 21-35;
Romans 14:13-23; 15:1-6;
Galatians 6:1-10;
Colossians 3:12-17;
1 John 4:7-12

Worrying about growing old
Psalm 37:23-29;
Isaiah 46:3-4

Worrying about money
Proverbs 11:7;
Ecclesiastes 5:10-20;
Matthew 6:24-34;
Luke 2:13-21;
1 Timothy 6:6-10

Worrying about the future
Isaiah 35; 60;
Jeremiah 29:10-14;
Peter 1:3-5;
Revelation 21:1-8

Experiencing Troublesome Feelings

Afraid?
Psalms 27; 91;
Isaiah 41:5-13;
Mark 4:35-41;
Hebrews 13:5-6;
1 John 4:13-18

Anxious? Worried?
Psalm 25;
Matthew 6:24-34;
Matthew 10:26-31;
1 Peter 1:3-5;
1 Peter 5:7

Afraid of death?
Psalm 23;
Psalm 63:1-8;
John 6:35-40;
Romans 8:18-39;
1 Corinthians 15:35-37;
2 Corinthians 5:1-10;
2 Timothy 1:8-10

Angry?
Proverbs 15:1;
Matthew 5:21-24;
Romans 12:17-21;
Ephesians 4:26-32;
James 1:19-21

Depressed?
Psalms 16:43; 130;
Isaiah 61:1-4;
Jeremiah 15:10-21;
Lamentations 3:55-57;
John 3:14-17;
Ephesians 3:14-21

Disappointed? Let down?
Psalm 55;
Psalm 62:1-8;
Jeremiah 20:7-18

Discouraged?
Psalm 34;
Isaiah 12:1-6
Romans 15:13;
2 Corinthians 4:16-18;
Philippians 4:10-13;
Colossians 1:9-14;
Hebrews 6:9-12

Doubting your faith in God?
Psalms 8; 145;
Proverbs 30:5;
Matthew 7:7-12;
Luke 17:5-6;
John 20:21-31;
Romans 4:13-25;
Hebrews 11;
1 John 5:13-15

Feeling useless? Inferior?
Isaiah 6:1-8;
Jeremiah 1:4-10;
Galatians 1:11-24;
Ephesians 2:1-16;
1 Peter 2:4-10

Frustrated?
Job 21:1-16;
Job 24:1-17;
Job 36:1-26;
Matthew 7:12, 14

Impatient?
Psalm 13;
Psalm 37:1-7;
Psalm 40:1-5;
Ecclesiastes 3:1-15;
Lamentations 3:25-33;
Hebrews 6:13-20;
James 5:7-11

Insecure? Lacking confidence?
Deuteronomy 31:1-8;
Psalms 73:21-26; 108;
Philippians 4:10-20;
1 John 3:19-24

Jealous?
Psalm 49;
Proverbs 23:17;
James 3:13-18

Lonely?
Psalms 22; 42;
John 14:15-31a

Overwhelmed? Experiencing stress?
Isaiah 55:1-9;
Matthew 11:25-30;
John 4:1-30;
2 Corinthians 6:3-10;
Revelation 22:17

Rejected?
Psalm 38;
Isaiah 52:13; 53:12;
Matthew 9:9-13;
Luke 4:16-30;
John 15:18–16:1a;
Ephesians 1:3-14;
1 Peter 2:1-10

Tempted?
Psalm 19:12-14;
Psalm 141;
Luke 4:1-13;
Hebrews 2:11-18;
Hebrews 4:14-16;
James 1:12-18

Tempted by sex?
2 Samuel 11:1-12, 25;
1 Corinthians 6:12-20;
Galatians 5:16-26

Tired? Weary?
Psalms 3:5-6; 4:4-8;
Isaiah 35:1-10;
Matthew 11:25-30;
2 Thessalonians 3:16;
Hebrews 4:1-11

Vengeful?
Matthew 5:38-42;
Romans 12:17-21

To me, there is no book in the world like the Bible. By believing its truths, persons have been transformed from wretched sinners into serving saints. Its words have brought comfort to grief-stricken hearts, courage to despairing souls, light to darkened pathways, and hope for the hopeless. Much of our best literature, music, poetry, and art have been influenced by its inspired message. Truly, the Bible is a book given to people and in-breathed by the Holy Spirit (see 2 Peter 1:21). Like the psalmist, I declare that His Word (the Bible) is "a lamp to my feet and a light to my path" (Psalm 119:105). Most important of all, the Bible reveals the perfect will of God in the words and deeds of Jesus Christ, our Savior and Lord!

Chapter III

Biblical Hermeneutics

(Guidelines for Interpreting the Bible)

At the close of chapter 1, we noted that the Bible is the Word of God; therefore, for it to be properly taught and proclaimed, one needs to be sure that one's teaching is biblically based, doctrinally sound, and life-centered. Now in this chapter, we will seek to reveal how one goes about accomplishing this task.

First, one must realize that the Bible is not an easy book to interpret. Of course, there are some statements in the Bible that are very obvious and their meanings are clear; but, as a whole, the Bible is not an easy book to interpret. Consequently, one needs solid and sound rules and principles to apply to the Bible in order to "rightly divide" or properly interpret it. That is what biblical hermeneutics is all about. It is often understood as the science of interpreting Scripture. A simple definition of biblical hermeneutics is that it is the study of those principles that pertain to the interpretation of Holy Scripture.

Since biblical hermeneutics focuses directly on the principles and guidelines of scriptural interpretation, let us delineate many of these principles so that we may discern more clearly how to understand and teach the Word of God.

I. GAPS BETWEEN US AND SCRIPTURE

We will do well to understand that one of the factors which makes the Bible difficult at points is that there are gaps which stand between us and it.

Historical Gap

There is a wide historical gap between Scripture and us. There are almost 2,000 years standing between us and the New Testament, and about 3,000 years standing between us and parts of the Old Testament. Moreover, the Bible was written over a 1,500-year period by many authors (66 books). Any time literary material is dated, one has to try to bridge the time gap in order to fully understand the material. Thus, the modern interpreter has to seek to bridge this historical gap. He or she has to search as carefully as possible to find the setting in life of a particular passage of Scripture. I will say more about this in a later section (see section on "When Was It Written").

Cultural Gap

The Palestinian culture was quite different from ours. For one thing, it was primarily agricultural in nature. Consequently, many of the ideas and illustrations were encased in agricultural language. For example, Jesus' parable of the Sower and Soils is specifically agricultural in nature. Thus, the interpreter would need some knowledge (whether he goes to Palestine or gains the information through reading biblical commentaries) of Palestinian soil to properly interpret this parable. For instance, when Jesus said that some of the seeds fell on rocky soil, He did not mean that it fell on soil that was mixed with many broken rocks. But rather, He meant that the soil had a layer of rocks underneath it, and when the Palestinian sun warmed the rock—because it was just beneath the topsoil—the seed would therefore quickly germinate. But it would die almost as quickly because the warm rock would block its ability to find depth in the soil.

Consequently, before applying this parable to our lives, one would need to understand this cultural factor. To illustrate the point further, observe the cultural peculiarity of the parable of the Ten Virgins. If one missed the point that weddings in Palestine were held basically at night, where there were no street lights—and therefore it was necessary for the virgins to be torch (lamp) bearers—one could therefore possibly miss the understanding of the passage and could proceed to give the wrong application.

Language Gap

Most of the Bible was written in the Hebrew, Aramaic, and Greek languages. Therefore, to understand some parts of the Bible, one either needs an understanding of these languages or some "biblical helps" where he or she can get the proper understanding and meaning of a particular text. For example, the Greek language has several words for love. They are *eros*, *agape*, and *philia*. And they do not all mean the same thing. For example, *eros* primarily deals with romantic love; *philia* primarily deals with love between brothers (sisters)—friendship love; and *agape* primarily deals with divine love, especially the love which God showed for us in allowing Jesus Christ to become the sacrificial Lamb for us at Calvary. Now, if one did not have an understanding of those shades of differences in these three Greek words for love, one could misinterpret John 21:15-17 where Jesus used both *agape* and *philia*, but our English version simply uses "love" for both Greek words. Hence, one could miss the shade of meaning here without an understanding of the Greek words used for "love" in this particular text.

Moreover, one must be aware of the linguistic idioms used in the Scripture. The Scriptures are filled with idioms. George M. Lamsa has written a book on *Idioms in the Bible Explained*.

Since these and other gaps exist between the Bible and us, they must be bridged by the interpreter in order to properly understand and correctly teach and proclaim the Word of God.

II. PERTINENT HERMENEUTICAL QUESTIONS

Not only should the teacher and preacher of Holy Scripture seek to bridge the gaps spoken of above, but also one needs to ask relevant and significant questions about the proper way to interpret Holy Scripture. Some years ago in a class in the Old Testament, Dr. J. Phillip Hyatt gave us some hermeneutical questions that have been very helpful to me. I share them with you. Dr. Hyatt said that we should raise the following questions when interpreting a verse, a paragraph, or any book(s) of the Bible:

*Who Wrote It?

This question obviously deals with the authorship of a book of the Bible. To understand who wrote a given book forces us to seek to learn something about the author's background and life. For example, understanding Paul's background is quite helpful in interpreting his letters. To understand his background in Judaism as a strict Pharisee and to know that he was converted to Christianity in an intense experience on the Damascus Road certainly sheds light on one's understanding of his letters. Thus, to know that Paul wrote a particular letter or epistle is to know that a Pauline "flavor" should be considered in one's interpretation. We could not connect Paul's statement in 2 Corinthians 5:17 ("Therefore if any man be in Christ, he is a new creature: old things are passed away; behold, all things are become new") without his Damascus Road experience.

Knowing the author helps in interpreting Scripture. The Ethiopian eunuch in Acts 8 raised a pertinent hermeneutical question when he asked Philip, "About whom does the prophet speak, himself or someone else?" Philip explained to the eunuch that the prophet had reference to Jesus. It is important for us to know in any given passage who is speaking and who is writing.

*When Was It Written?

This hermeneutic question focuses on the historical setting of the passage of Scripture or book of the Bible. This is probably one of the most crucial questions of all because it helps us to place a passage in the right time frame and historical location. We can better understand and apply the biblical material if we know when it was spoken or written.

For example, scholars remind us that in the Old Testament prophetic period, we can talk about a pre-exilic, an exilic, and a post-exilic period. Therefore, when a certain prophetic book is interpreted, we need to know whether the prophet was addressing a pre-exilic audience, an exilic audience, or a post-exilic audience. For example, Isaiah has material in his book that is pre-exilic, exilic, and post-exilic. Usually, scholars think of chapters 1–39 as being pre-exilic and the chapters that follow as exilic and post-exilic. To place chapter 40 of Isaiah in the pre-exilic period would cause the interpretation to lose much of its flavor, power, and meaning. Consequently, if one lifts a passage out of its historical setting (historical location in life), then one is likely to misrepresent its application for our modern situation.

Take Ezekiel for example. He was primarily an exilic prophet. He ministered to the Jewish people during their Babylonian exile. Thus, if one tries to interpret Ezekiel 37 apart from Babylonian exile, one will not only miss the historical setting and historical meaning, but he or she may also misapply the text for our modern usage and application.

The historical setting of the Bible also causes us to look at book sequence. Many of the books of the Bible are not in historical sequence (chronology). In the Old Testament, Ezra and Nehemiah are out of chronological order. They are both post-exilic books but are listed among the pre-exilic books. So the careful student of the Bible will need to study to know this fact, and will consequently place these books in their proper historical setting so that their messages can be properly interpreted, "rightly divided," and correctly applied.

*Why Was It Written?

Here the student of Scripture is concerned with finding the author's original intent. He or she is using the best methods to ascertain the meaning and purpose that the prophet had in mind when he wrote the book of Isaiah, that Paul had in mind when he wrote 1 and 2 Corinthians, and his other letters.

To arrive at the best intent of the original author, one has to do sound exegesis. "Exegesis" is from a Greek word that means to get out of a passage that which is therein. It is, as someone has noted, the opposite of *eisegesis*—to read into the text one's own opinion. Thus, if the true intent of the original author is to be understood, one must dig with spiritual eyes and heart, as well as with the best Bible translations, the best commentaries, and other biblical tools and aids in order to ascertain the truth of the passage (see chapter on "Tools and Aids for Bible Study"). When one has done thorough exegesis and has lifted out the true meaning of the text (passage of Scripture), then he or she is ready to do relevant application of the Scripture.

One cannot do proper application and exposition until proper exegesis has been done. In exegesis, the teacher focuses on the historical meaning of the passage of Scripture. In exposition and application, one focuses on the relevance of the passage for this generation. Let us be sure that we understand that both of these methods must be done. Exegesis cannot be divorced from application, nor can application be divorced form exegesis. They are two parts of a whole.

There have been periods in our society when persons have done sound and thorough exegesis, but have failed to apply the passage of Scripture to the current generation. Always, after we have done our exegesis, we must then apply it to our current spiritual, social, political, racial, economic, moral, and ecological lives. We must teach relevantly and holistically. The Word of God, in exegesis and application, must be brought to bear on the whole person and society. Consequently, when proper exegesis is done, one can arrive at a clearer understanding of the purpose of the text or book of the Bible for individuals and culture.

Suppose one raises the question, "What was the purpose of the author of the gospel of John?" Fortunately, the answer is in the Gospel itself. In John 20:30-31, the author declares, "Now Jesus did many other signs in the presence of his disciples, which are not written in this book; but these are written that you may believe that Jesus is the Christ, the Son of God, and that believing you may have life in his name" (RSV). And so John's purpose is to give theological photographs of Jesus so people may see that He is the Son of God and may therefore make a decision for or against Jesus as their Savior and Lord.

I indicated earlier Paul's purpose for writing 1 and 2 Corinthians. A careful reading of these letters reveals that he was writing to a young church troubled with many problems and puzzled by many theological questions. Paul wrote these letters to answer many of their questions (one of his pet phrases is "now concerning..." this or that...) (see 1 Corinthians 12:1, etc.), and to encourage them in the Lord toward a fuller Christian commitment and a higher level of Christian morality.

If one raised the question of the purpose of the author of the apocalyptic book of Revelation, what should be the answer? Of course, depending on who is speaking or writing, the answer to this question would vary. But the most practical answer is that the author of Revelation wrote to say to a group of persecuted Christians, "Hold on, don't give up; be encouraged in the Lord, because God is going to win, not Caesar." The theme verse is Revelation 11:15: "Then the seventh angel blew his trumpet, and there were loud voices in heaven, saying, 'The kingdom of the world has become the kingdom of our Lord and of his Messiah, and he will reign forever and ever'" (NRSV). Everything else written in the book of Revelation must pivot on this theme if the purpose of the author of the book is to be correctly interpreted and applied.

*To Whom Was It Written?

This question is significant because we carefully focus on the conditions and circumstances of the recipients of the letters and epistles. Let us use the book of Revelation again as an illustration. To whom did John write the book of Revelation? He wrote it to a group of people undergoing persecution at the hands of the Roman Emperor. Thus, the condition of the people of the book was one of severe persecution.

When writing to people gripped in the throes of a hostile government, one probably would not risk writing to them in plain and ordinary language. Rather, he or she would probably write to them in symbolic, figurative, and code language. It would be written in a way that they (the persecuted ones) could understand, but not the enemies (the emperor and his henchmen). This is precisely what John did in the book of Revelation. He wrote much of the book in "hidden" and code language. In fact, the Greek word for "Revelation" is *apocalypse,* which means, "an uncovering." Therefore, the book of Revelation was a "covered" (hidden) message to the enemy (the Roman Empire), but an uncovered message to the persecuted Christians. Because the message was coded, symbolic, and hidden to the enemy, they did not burn and destroy the scroll as they did Jeremiah's prophecies (see Jeremiah 36). And so, through coded, symbolic, and figurative language, God sent His message through John to the persecuted churches in the Roman Empire. Now, if this point is overlooked, one can easily miss the intent of the book of Revelation and, therefore, grossly misinterpret it.

III. THE INTERPRETIVE PRINCIPLES AND OTHER LITERARY FORMS

Just as the book of Revelation is primarily apocalyptic in nature and contains coded, symbolic, and figurative language that is common to it, the second half of Daniel and the second half of Zechariah contain other literary forms (literary expressions) of biblical literature that need to be discussed.

These expressions are metaphors, similes, analogies, hyperboles, anthropomorphic terms, parables, poetry, and prophetic literature. Since these figures of speech and literary forms are not to be taken literally, the interpreter of Scripture needs a general understanding of each form of speech and literary style in order to arrive at the true meaning of a biblical passage where these forms are used.

Metaphors

The *Reader's Digest Dictionary* states that a metaphor is a figure of speech in which one object is likened to another by speaking of it as if it were the other, as in the sentence "He was a lion in battle," or as in the phrase "evening of life." There are many metaphorical expressions in the Bible, and the student must recognize and interpret them accordingly. For example, Jesus says metaphorically, "You are the light of the world," suggesting that Christian disciples should influence the world the way light influences darkness. We should be dispellers and extinguishers of moral and spiritual darkness. Paul used beautiful and cogent metaphors as he wrote in Ephesians 6, "Put on the whole armour of God...the breastplate of righteousness...the shield of faith...the helmet of salvation, and the sword of the Spirit, which is the word of God" (11a, 14b, 16, KJV).

Simile

The *Reader's Digest Great Encyclopedic Dictionary* states that a simile is a figure of speech expressing comparison or likeness by the use of such terms as like, as, so, etc. This dictionary further suggests that a metaphor differs from a simile only in omitting "like" or "as" as words of comparison. For example, "an alpine peak like a frosted cake" is a simile. In the New Testament, a simile is employed when Jesus said, "Behold I send you forth as sheep in the midst of wolves." Here He compares the Christian disciples with sheep. We are not sheep, but we are like sheep. We are sent out into a world to minister wherein we will be vulnerable to satanic enemies just as sheep are vulnerable to wolves. However, we have the Good Shepherd's protective care.

Analogy

The Bible contains many analogies. An analogy is an expression that denotes similarity of one thing to another in terms of function or position. For example, Paul used the analogy (1 Corinthians 12) of the church as the body of Christ, using the human body to make his point vivid. The author of 1 Peter used analogies to speak about the church. He says, "But you are a chosen generation, a royal priesthood, a holy nation, His own special people, that you may proclaim the praises of Him who called you out of darkness into His marvelous light; who once were not a people but are now the people of God, who had not obtained mercy but now have obtained mercy" (1 Peter 2:9-10, NKJV).

Hyperbole

A hyperbole is an exaggerated expression or statement used to make a point. For example, the following are hyperbolas:

"I could sleep for a year."
"This book weighs a ton."
"I am starving to death."

In Matthew 7:3, Jesus used a hyperbole when He said, "And why beholdest thou the mote that is in thy brother's eye, but considerest not the beam that is in thine own eye?" (KJV). Here, Jesus was emphasizing the point that we should not judge our fellow human beings but should allow God, who is perfect, to be their judge. And so, He exaggerated the point by saying that the person with the log in his eye certainly should not try to judge the person who has saw dust (a speck) in his eye. Who could miss the fact that this is a hyperbole that makes a graphic point?

Again in Matthew 23:24, Jesus used a hyperbole: "You blind guides, straining out a gnat and swallowing a camel" (RSV). Of course, Jesus did not mean that the Pharisees ate the whole camel, hair, hump, and hoof! No, He was suggesting to them that they majored in minor things. He was rebuking them for being concerned about small transgressions of their petty rules while showing little or no regard for God's major principles of justice and righteousness.

Therefore, when interpreting the Word of God, one should allow hyperbolas to be hyperbolas and not take them literally. They are figures of speech used to teach a truth.

Anthropomorphic Terms

Whenever someone ascribes a human characteristic to God, he or she is speaking of God in anthropomorphic language. God is a Spiritual Being. But we talk about Him in human terms (anthropomorphic terms). We say that He walks and talks, rides and hears. The writer of Genesis is using anthropomorphic language when he says that Adam and Eve heard the Lord God walking in the garden in the cool day (Genesis 3:8). Isaiah also speaks anthropomorphically. He says about God, "He shall feed his flock like a shepherd: he shall gather the lambs with his arm, and carry them in his bosom, and shall gently lead those that are with young" (Isaiah 40:11, KJV). Thus, Isaiah pictures God as having arms and a bosom, and He walks before His children. We know that Isaiah is simply picturing God in human terms. There are many, many more examples, but these should suffice.

The Parable

The Parable is another vehicle of expression used for teaching purposes. It is commonly defined as an earthly story (illustration) with a heavenly meaning. Some think of a parable as an extended metaphor or simile that compares a religious truth with a common experience or circumstance in life. Jesus is perhaps the master at using this method for didactic purposes. In fact, most of Jesus' lessons on the kingdom of God are encouched in parabolic form. (See Matthew 13 and 25 as examples.)

Now, when one is interpreting parables, he or she should keep in mind that parables have central points; and one should find the central point of the parable and not get bogged down in the peripheral concerns in the parable. Many interpreters take too seriously the simple details of the parable rather than concentrating on its "big truth" or central idea. (See the chapter on "How to Prepare a Lesson.") Colson offers the following four helpful principles when seeking to interpret a parable:

1. Be sure you understand the language of the parable itself, and its allusions to social customs or physical facts.
2. Ascertain what subject the parable is intended to illustrate. Remember that a parable is always an illustration of a spiritual truth. Most of the time, the context will indicaten what subject is being dealt with, or what truth is being illustrated.
3. Note what light the parable as a whole throws upon the subject—that is, what aspects of the truth it particularly illustrates.
4. Decide how far you may regard the separate details as carrying special significance. The details must always be subordinate to the main point; in all pictorial representation, there is much that is mere setting or costume. Do not try to find a special meaning in every detail unless the content so indicates. Occasionally, Jesus did put meaning into the specific details, as in Matthew 13:24-30 (as interpreted in verses 36-43). But His application of the parable of the Good Samaritan (Luke 10:37) makes nothing of the details; only the main point is emphasized. Actually, there are some parables in which it would be quite impossible to find every detail corresponding to some spiritual reality.[1]

Hebrew Poetry

Most people are aware that poetry has its own uniqueness when compared with prose. Likewise, Hebrew poetry has its own unique flavor. In the early days of American poetry, we saw a great deal of rhyme. Rhyme seemed to improve people's memory. In fact, much of our hymn singing is filled with rhyme and, therefore, is easier to remember. While Hebrew poetry is characterized by rhythm, it very seldom rhymes. In fact, we learned in Old Testament classes that one of the chief characteristics of Hebrew poetry is PARALLELISM. That is, the second line of the couplet or verse may repeat the thought of the first line with different words:

> Wash me thoroughly from my iniquity, and cleanse me from my sin! (Psalm 51:2, RSV)

The second line may complete the idea given in the first line:

> He only is my rock and my salvation, my fortress: I shall not be greatly moved. (Psalm 62:2, RSV)

The second line of a verse or couplet may present a contrasting thought:

> A man's spirit will endure sickness; but a broken spirit who can bear? (Proverbs 18:14, RSV)

Unless the interpreter of Scripture is aware of these characteristics of poetic parallelism, he or she may read more into a passage than is really there. For example, I once heard a student interpret Psalm 51:5—a statement that represents parallelism—and he found far more in the passage than was intended. He sought to give a long discourse on the difference between sin and iniquity when in fact the psalmist was using them interchangeably. And so, when one is interpreting the Bible, he or she must be aware of the various figures of speech and language usage, giving serious attention to the uniqueness of each vehicle of expression as it impacts the meaning of a passage of Scripture.

Prophetic Literature

Many people misunderstand and misapply prophetic literature because they do not clearly understand the nature and function of a prophet. They often mix up general prophetic literature with apocalyptic literature. Earlier I mentioned that much of the books of Daniel, Zechariah, and Revelation are apocalyptic literature—that is, literature that was written during periods of severe persecution of God's people. Thus, the writings were encouched in symbols, codes, and figurative language. And to properly interpret this literature, one must seek to unlock the symbols, codes, and figures of speech. In this same light, many people think that Daniel and Revelation are general prophetic books. They are not. They are basically apocalyptic books and must be interpreted by the rules and guidelines of apocalyptic literature.

On the other hand, general prophetic literature has its own flavor of interpretation. One can best interpret prophetic literature by understanding the definition and function of a prophet. A prophet in the Old Testament was primarily a spokesman for God. He received his word from God through direct revelation, visions, dreams, etc., and then he would thunder "Thus saith the Lord" to the people of his day. In other words, a prophet received his message from God and delivered it to His people. Contrary to popular opinion, prophets were not predictors and foretellers of the future. Rather, they were persons who received messages from God that dealt primarily with the times and circumstances in which the people were living. Prophets then were very much like preachers today. They received and applied the Word of God to situations in their own generation. When one reads Isaiah, Amos, Hosea, Jeremiah, and other "major" prophets, he or she will discover that very little of what they said had to do with the future. What they received from God had primarily, I repeat, to do with their then present-day situations. To be sure, there are some matters in their prophecies that pointed to the future (Messianic prophecies, etc.). But the larger portion of their writings had to do with situations relative to the life and conduct of Israel, Judah, and the surrounding nations.

Thus, when one interprets prophetic literature with this understanding, he or she does not run the risk of applying things and events that applied specifically to that day and time to our day and time. Too many people see Russia and America and other nations in biblical prophecy when the prophet initially did not have these nations in mind at all. Now, of course, the Word of God in the prophetic books can be applied to Russia, America, etc. But these were not the original peoples whom the prophet was addressing. Originally, the prophet was addressing God's people, then: Israel, Judah, and the surrounding nations. After we correctly interpret the prophet's message to the people of that day, then we can move on to interpret it correctly for our day. As stated previously, historical exegesis must precede modern application.

IV. HERMENEUTICS AND THE MEANING OF THE REVELATION OF JESUS CHRIST

The Bible is the written Word of God given through many human authors to mankind. What is most pivotal for Christians is that within the written Word of God is the LIVING WORD of God—Jesus the Christ (John 1:14); and He makes all the difference in the interpretive process. Some scholars speak about a doctrine called progressive revelation. Simply stated, this doctrine emphasizes that God progressively revealed Himself to mankind in the Bible culminating in His revelation of Himself in Jesus Christ. Thus, all that God has revealed in the Bible must finally be viewed through the supreme revelation of God in Jesus Christ.

This truth, then, makes the New Testament (New Covenant) more authoritative for Christians than some parts of the Old Testament (Old Covenant). There are several passages of Scripture that support this position:

    A.   God, who at various times and in different ways spoke in time past to the fathers by the prophets, has in these last days spoken to us by His Son, whom He has appointed heir of all things, through whom also He made the worlds; who being the brightness of His glory and the express image of His person, and upholding all things by the word of His power, when He had by Himself purged our sins, sat down at the right hand of the Majesty on high. (Hebrews 1:1-3, NKJV)

            For on the one hand there is an annulling of the former commandment because of its weakness and unprofitableness. (Hebrews 7:18, NKJV)

            But now He has obtained a more excellent ministry, inasmuch as He is also Mediator of a better covenant, which was established on better promises. For if that first covenant had been faultless, then no place would have been sought for a second. Because finding fault with them, He says: "Behold, the days are coming, says the LORD, when I will make a new covenant with the house of Israel and with the house of Judah—not according to the covenant that I made with their fathers in the day when I took them by the hand to lead them out of the land of Egypt; because they did not continue in My covenant, and I disregarded them, says the LORD. For this is the covenant that I will make with the house of Israel after those days, says the LORD: I will put My laws in their mind and write them on their hearts; and I will be their God, and they shall be My people. None of them shall teach his neighbor, and none his brother, saying, 'Know the LORD,' for all shall know Me, from the least of them to the greatest of them. For I will be merciful to their unrighteousness, and their sins and their lawless deeds I will remember no more." In that He says, "A new covenant," He has made the first obsolete. Now what is becoming obsolete and growing old is ready to vanish away. (Hebrews 8:6-13, NKJV)

B. Ye have heard that it was said of them of old time, Thou shalt not kill; and whosoever shall kill shall be in danger of the judgment: But I say unto you, That whosoever is angry with his brother without a cause shall be in danger of the judgment: and whosoever shall say to his brother, Raca, shall be in danger of the council: but whosoever shall say, Thou fool, shall be in danger of hell fire. (Matthew 5:21-22, KJV)

Ye have heard that it was said by them of old time, Thou shalt not commit adultery: But I say unto you, That whosoever looketh on a woman to lust after her hath committed adultery with her already in his heart. (Matthew 5:27-28, KJV)

Again, ye have heard that it hath been said by them of old time, Thou shalt not forswear thyself, but shalt perform unto the Lord thine oaths: But I say unto you, Swear not at all; neither by heaven; for it is God's throne: Nor by the earth; for it is his footstool: neither by Jerusalem; for it is the city of the great King. (Matthew 5:33-35, KJV)

Ye have heard that it hath been said, An eye for an eye, and a tooth for a tooth: But I say unto you, That ye resist not evil: but whosoever shall smite thee on thy right cheek, turn to him the other also. (Matthew 5:38-39, KJV)

> Ye have heard that it hath been said, Thou shalt love thy neighbour, and hate thine enemy. But I say unto you, Love your enemies, bless them that curse you, do good to them that hate you, and pray for them which despitefully use you, and persecute you; That ye may be the children of your Father which is in heaven: for he maketh his sun to rise on the evil and on the good, and sendeth rain on the just and on the unjust. (Matthew 5:43-45, KJV)

C. Beware lest any man spoil you through philosophy and vain deceit, after the tradition of men, after the rudiments of the world, and not after Christ. For in him dwelleth all the fulness of the Godhead bodily. And ye are complete in him, which is the head of all principality and power. (Colossians 2:8-10, KJV)

All of these passages clearly indicate that in the coming of Christ and His teachings, the revelation of God has been updated. In Hebrews 1:1-3, the writer emphatically states that God has given His final and decisive revelation of Himself in Jesus Christ. In the Matthean passages, one cannot miss the pivotal words of Christ: "You have heard that it was said to them of old…But I say unto you…." Christ is declaring that what was said of old (revealed in the Old Covenant) must now be updated by Him in order for it to be the full revelation of God. That is why all Scripture must be finally measured by the standards, principles, and ethics of Jesus, the Christ of God. In other words, until we understand and teach Scripture from Christ's perspective, we are teaching at a sub-Christian level. I repeat, all Scriptures must be measured by His revelation of God, His understanding of God, and His teachings about the kingdom of God. Therefore, no doctrinal principle for interpreting the Bible is more important than the understanding that Jesus is the full and final revelation of God. God has spoken His final and full biblical word in Jesus, the living Word.

V. OTHER HERMENEUTICAL RULES

A. Read the Bible as a whole. That is, read each verse in relationship to the paragraph, read each paragraph in relationship to the chapter, read each chapter in relationship to the whole book, and read the whole book in relationship to the whole Bible. This helps prevent one from taking passages out of their contexts. Every verse in the Bible has a particular context and must be first interpreted in that particular context, and then in the larger context of the whole Bible. One of the particular characteristics of sects and cults is that they take Scripture out of its context. One can make the Bible say almost anything he or she wants it to say when Scripture is interpreted out of its context. I remember the story a professor shared regarding this issue when I was in college. He said a person could prove by the Bible that one should hang himself. He quoted the passage in which Judas hanged himself. Then he turned to the passage in which Jesus said to the young Ruler, "Go thou and do likewise." Thus he said, if one took these two passages out of context and joined them, one could prove biblically that one should hang himself. In this same light, reading chapters and books of the Bible is like reading a letter from a friend. No one reads part of a letter and accepts it as the whole letter. Likewise, we should read a whole chapter and book before seeking to interpret its parts.

B. Read, study, and teach the Bible in the power of the Holy Spirit. The Holy Spirit should always be invited into our Bible reading and study periods, our lesson preparation, and our teaching sessions. We should keep this principle in mind because the Holy Scriptures were written by persons divinely inspired by God. Paul had this truth in mind when he wrote 1 Corinthians 2:13-14a,16:

> These things we also speak, not in words which man's wisdom teaches but which the Holy Spirit teaches, comparing spiritual things with spiritual. But the natural man does not receive the things of the Spirit of God, ... For "who has known the mind of the LORD that he may instruct Him?" But we have the mind of Christ. (NKJV)

NOTE

1. Howard P. Colson, *Preparing to Teach the Bible* (Nashville, Tennessee: Convention Press, 1959), 61-62.

Chapter IV

Tools and Aids for Bible Study and Bible Teaching

In an earlier chapter, I mentioned that the Bible was not an easy book to read and understand. Consequently, it is necessary to ascertain the best tools and aids one can find in order to understand and teach the Bible. First, let us make a general comment about background for solid and effective teaching. It is most appropriate for each teacher to have a good theological education from a college of the Bible or a seminary. In seminary, one can study Bible and Theology, Church History, Christian Ministries, Church and Society, Christian Ethics, Preaching and Christian Worship, Christian Education, and the like. Most church schoolteachers are not fortunate enough to acquire this wide background in theological education. Even so, they should prepare themselves by using the best tools, aids, and methods available. Just as a carpenter does his best work when he has the best tools, likewise, Christian church schoolteachers will do their best work when they avail themselves to the best biblical tools and aids.

The teacher should develop a clear, overall understanding of the Old and New Testaments. I always recommend that people begin with the New Testament, probably with the Gospels, then Acts, then the letters, epistles, and the book of Revelation. Of course, in the Old Testament, one should read the Law (first five books), then the prophets, the historical books, and, finally, the Wisdom Literature. In order for one to accomplish this task, one must discipline oneself to daily reading and study of the Bible.

What forms of help are there for one to better understand and teach the Bible? First, one needs a good study Bible. Colson referred to this Bible as a "teacher's Bible."[1]

A good study Bible will contain valuable help. You would want a Bible with a small dictionary and concordance—one which offers help with pronunciation of words, one which has maps of the Bible lands, and one which has introductions to each book of the Bible.

Bible Translations

I firmly believe that a Bible student needs more than one translation of the Bible. Good Bible translations help one to understand word usage, especially since word meanings change over a period of time. Many people read the King James Version which was translated in AD 1611. Since that time, many words have changed in meaning; therefore, a more modern translation would aid one in Bible study.

Many people, even in this modern period, are not aware that the King James Version of the Bible did not come directly from God. They swear by the Holy Bible (meaning the King James Version) as though there are no other good translations of the Bible. In fact, I have heard well-meaning Christians refer to current translations as "man-made Bibles," meaning that any translation other than the King James Version (1611) is not of God. For people who think this way, it is good for us to look at the following bird's-eye view of the history of Bible translations:

1. Original Bible on scrolls
   Old Testament in Hebrew and Aramaic
   New Testament in Greek
2. Septuagint (about 250 BC)
   Greek Old Testament
3. Vulgate (about AD 400)
   Latin translation
4. Wycliffe Bible, AD 1384
   English Translation
5. Tyndale Bible, AD 1530
   English Version

6. Luther's Bible, AD 1534
   German Translation
7. Coverdale Bible, AD 1535
   English Translation
8. Geneva Bible, AD 1560
9. Douay Version, AD 1610
   English Catholic Bible
10. King James Version, AD 1611
11. English Revised Version, AD 1885
12. American Standard Version, AD 1901
13. Revised Standard Version, AD 1952
14. New American Standard Version, AD 1966
15. Jerusalem Bible, AD 1966
16. The New English Bible, AD 1970
17. New American Bible, AD 1970
18. The Living Bible, AD 1971
19. Good News Bible, AD 1976
20. New International Version, AD 1979
21. New King James Version, AD 1982
22. Reader's Digest Bible, AD 1982
23. New Revised Standard Version, AD 1991

This is not an exhaustive list of modern translations. There are many more, but these are the major ones.

King James Version

Without a doubt, this English version has been one of the most popular translations in the history of the Bible. Translated in AD 1611 and authorized by King James of England, it has been praised for its beautiful and majestic style. It is still, perhaps, read by more English-speaking people than any other version.

Although the King James Version is still popular and valuable, it does have its shortcomings. First, the English language has changed tremendously since AD 1611. Reading some parts of the King James Version is as difficult as reading the literature of William Shakespeare, who lived and wrote about the same time as the birth of the

King James Version. Take the word *prevent* as an example. In AD 1611, *prevent* meant to "come before," but today, *prevent* means "to stop someone from doing something." In that light, let us look at a verse from Psalm 119:147:

> I prevented the dawning of the morning, and cried: I hoped in thy word." (KJV)

The Revised Standard Version renders this verse as follows:

> I rise before dawn and cry for help; I hope in thy words.

When the King James Version was translated in AD 1611, the word *prevent* meant "come before." Thus, in the King James Version, the psalmist was saying that he rose before the dawn. But hardly anyone today would read the King James Version of this passage and understand that the word *prevent* means "to come before or rise before." This verse is, however, made very clear in the Revised Standard Version rendering. The same point can be seen in 1 Thessalonians 4:15 (KJV): "For this we say unto you by the word of the Lord, that we which are alive and remain unto the coming of the Lord shall not prevent them which are asleep." From the modern usage of "prevent, one would think from the King James Version rendering of this passage that those who are alive will stop those who are asleep from rising from the dead to be with the Lord! But *prevent,* here, means (as in Psalm 119:147) "to come before." Thus, the true meaning of the passage is that those who are alive at the coming of Christ will not get ahead of those Christians who are dead. The Revised Standard Version rightly renders this verse: "For this we declare to you by the word of the Lord, that we who are alive, who are left until the coming of the Lord, shall not precede those who have fallen asleep."

Another weakness of the King James Version of the Bible is that it does not always identify poetry from prose. Compare Isaiah 5:1-7 in the King James Version with Isaiah 5:1-7 in the Revised Version.

King James Version	**Revised Standard Version**
NOW WILL I sing to my wellbeloved a song of my beloved touching his vineyard. My wellbeloved hath a vineyard in a very fruitful hill:	LET ME sing for my beloved a love song concerning his vineyard: My beloved had a vineyard on a very fertile hill.
2 And he fenced it, and gathered out the stones thereof, and planted it with the choicest vine, and built a tower in the midst of it, and also made a winepress therein: and he looked that it should bring forth grapes, and it brought forth wild grapes.	2 He digged it and cleared it of stones, and planted it with choice vines; he built a watchtower in the midst of it, and hewed out a wine vat in it; and he looked for it to yield grapes, but it yielded wild grapes.
3 And now, O inhabitants of Jerusalem, and men of Judah, judge, I pray you, betwixt me and my vineyard.	3 And now, O inhabitants of Jerusalem and men of Judah, judge, I pray you, between me and my vineyard.
4 What could have been done more to my vineyard, that I have not done in it? wherefore, when I looked that it should bring forth grapes, brought it forth wild grapes?	4 What more was there to do for my vineyard, that I have not done in it? When I looked for it to yield grapes, why did it yield wild grapes?
5 And now go to; I will tell you what I will do to my vineyard: I will take away the hedge thereof, and it shall be eaten up; and break down the wall thereof, and it shall be trodden down:	5 And now I will tell you what I will do to my vineyard. I will remove its hedge, and it shall be devoured; I will break down its wall, and it shall be trampled down.
6 And I will lay it waste: it shall not be pruned, nor digged; but there shall come up briers and thorns: I will also command the clouds that they rain no rain upon it.	6 I will make it a waste; it shall not be pruned or hoed, and briers and thorns shall grow up; I will also command the clouds that they rain no rain upon it.
7 For the vineyard of the LORD of hosts is the house of Israel, and the men of Judah his pleasant plant: and he looked for judgment, but behold oppression; for righteousness, but behold a cry.	7 For the vineyard of the LORD of hosts is the house of Israel, and the men of Judah are his pleasant planting; and he looked for justice, but behold, bloodshed; for righteousness, but behold, a cry!

The Revised Standard Version is set in poetical style, while the King James Version is written in prose.

Moreover, the King James Version does not utilize quotation marks to identify quotes. Compare Matthew 8:2 and 8:4 in the King James Version with the same passage in the Revised Standard Version.

And, behold, there came a leper and worshipped him, saying, Lord, if thou wilt, thou canst make me clean. (8:2, KJV)

And behold, a leper came to him and knelt before him, saying, "Lord, if you will, you can make me clean." (8:2, RSV)

And Jesus saith unto him, See thou tell no man; but go thy way, show thyself to the priest, and offer the gift that Moses commanded, for a testimony unto them. (8:4, KJV)

And Jesus said to him, "See that you say nothing to any one; but go, show yourself to the priest, and offer the gift that Moses commanded, for a proof to the people." (8:4, RSV)

In this light, it is very clear to me that if one chooses to use the King James Version of the Bible, one should consult current translations to arrive at a clearer understanding of the text. Thus, if one loves the style and beauty of the King James Version, it would be very helpful to use a New King James Version along with it. Or you may want to use the Revised Standard Version or the American Standard Version, both of which scholars agree to be good translations from the original Greek and Hebrew texts. If you are looking for a more recent conservative English translation, many scholars suggest the New International Version. Also, the Revised Standard Version (1952) has been updated. It is now called the New Revised Standard Version. Many seminary professors are already singing its praises.[2]

Dictionaries of the Bible

Serious students of the Bible will always have their Bible dictionary nearby as they study the Scripture. A Bible dictionary is a valuable tool because it contains not only definitions of words and theological terms, but it also gives information on books of the Bible (their historical backgrounds, etc.), recent archaeological findings, and the like. Here is a brief listing of some valuable Bible dictionaries:

1. *The Westminster Dictionary of the Bible*, 1944
2. *Harper's Bible Dictionary*, 1952

3. *The Interpreter's Dictionary of the Bible* (four volumes)
4. *The New Bible Dictionary*, 1962
5. *Unger's Bible Dictionary*
6. *Hasting's Dictionary of the Bible*, edited by F. C. Grant and H. H. Rowley, 1963
7. *A Theological Wordbook of the Bible*, edited by Alan Richardson, 1950
8. *An Expository Dictionary of Biblical Words* (W. E. Vine)
9. *The Zondervan Pictorial Encyclopedia of the Bible* (five volumes)

Concordances of the Bible

Have you ever longed to find a verse in the Bible and could not? Did you, after spending hours, finally call a friend who helped you find the verse? A good concordance could have saved you a lot of time because a complete concordance lists all the major words in the Bible in sequential order of the books of the Bible. Thus, if you can remember only one word in a verse, you can go to your concordance and look up that word and the concordance will tell you where to find the specific book, chapter, and verse that you are looking for. For example, if you could not remember where the verse is that says "Jesus wept," all you would need to do is turn in your concordance to the word *wept* and follow it down to John's gospel and it would point you to the exact chapter and verse for which you are looking. This little tool has saved many a teacher and preacher hours that otherwise would have been wasted looking for a particular passage.

Listed below are some of the best complete concordances of the Bible:
- *Cruden's Complete Concordance*
- *Young's Analytical Concordance to the Bible*
- *Strong's Exhaustive Concordance of the Bible*

For more current translations of the Bible, there are corresponding concordances.

Bible Commentaries

This is another important tool for Bible study. A good commentary gives the history and background of a book of the Bible and the date and authorship, along with other helpful theological insights. It also gives a verse-by-verse explanation of the text, called by many the exegesis of the text. Finally, a good commentary gives an exposition or application of the text, which helps one to understand its modern-day meaning and application. Here is a brief listing of some helpful commentaries on the Bible:

- *The Broadman Bible Commentary*
- *The International Critical Commentary*
- *Matthew Henry's Commentary*
- *The Wycliffe Bible Commentary*
- *Peake's Bible Commentary,* edited by Black & Rowley
- *The Layman's Bible Commentary*
- *William Barclay's Commentary on the New Testament*
- *The Abingdon Bible Commentary*
- *The New Bible Commentary*
- *Word Biblical Commentary*

Bible Atlases

An atlas of the Bible can help one identify places and people in their proper perspective. The following four are valuable:
1. *The Westminster Historical Atlas of the Bible* (Revised Edition), 1956
2. *The Oxford Bible Atlas*
3. *Baker Bible Atlas*
4. *The Rand McNally Bible Atlas*

Biblical Archaeology

Biblical archaeology can also be a valuable tool for the serious student of the Bible. In its simplest form, biblical archaeology is the study of the material remains of places and cultures relative to biblical people and events. This scientific study helps one to have a greater understanding of the times, events, and people recorded in the Bible. For many years, archaeologists have been scientifically excavating and studying the material remains of cultures and events in Palestine, Egypt, Assyria, Asia Minor, Macedonia, Greece, Rome, and the like.

How do these archaeological excavations and discoveries help the student of the Bible? Olin T. Binkley answers this question in a very cogent way as he reflects on documents (The Black Obelisk, Moabite Stone, Babylonian Chronicle, Code of Hammurabi, etc.) found in lands of the Bible. He writes the following:

> Meaning of Words: The documents make the Bible more intelligible by providing the previously unknown meaning of many words and phrases. For example, in Hosea 3:2, a word is used which does not occur elsewhere in the Old Testament. The word is *lethech*, and is used for a particular measure of barley. Since the word appeared nowhere else, Bible scholars felt that the text was in error and should be changed. But in two texts from Ugarit, the word was used, as it was in Hosea, to describe a unit of dry measure—although the size is not definitely stated.
>
> A Hebrew word, *miqweh*, occurs in 1 Kings 10:28, in a description of Solomon's trading activity; but, the meaning of the word has been unknown. The King James Version translates the word as "linen yarn": "And Solomon had horses brought out of Egypt, and linen yarn: the king's merchants received the linen yarn at a price." The American Standard Version has "droves": "And the horses which received them in droves, each drove at a price." Assyrian records indicate that the word must refer to a place, *Kue*, in Asia Minor. This is the translation of the Revised Standard Version, therefore: "And Solomon's import of horses was from Egypt and *Kue*, and the king's traders received them from *Kue* at a price."
>
> A group of names appearing in 2 Kings 18:17; Jeremiah 39:13, and elsewhere were translated in the King James Version as personal names of individuals—*Tartan, Rabshekeh, Rabsaris,* and *Rabmag.* Assyrian inscriptions show that these words are actually titles of Assyrian officials. *Tartan* is the "commander-in-chief," *Rabshakehi* is probably the "field marshal," *Rabsaris* is

perhaps the "chief eunuch," and *Rabmag* is apparently some other high official.[3]

He also explains how archaeology helps us understand laws, customs, and religious practices in the Bible:

> Illustration of Practices: Another important value lies in the illustration of laws, customs, and religious practices mentioned in the Bible. Many of these practices have been obscure.
>
> In Deuteronomy 14:21, there is a command, "You shall not boil a kid in its mother's milk" (RSV). There is no apparent reason for this law, and students have sought some logical explanation for it. In the Ras Shamra literature is reference in a poem concerning cooking a kid in milk, and it is practically certain that this was a Canaanite religious rite. The law in Deuteronomy is a forceful way of telling the Israelites not to practice pagan religious rites.
>
> In Genesis 16, Sarah gives her servant Hagar to Abraham in order that she might bear him a son. Is this an isolated case, or is this a common practice? In the Code of Hammurabi is evidence that this was a common practice. It provides that a handmaid who has been given by a wife to a husband and has borne him children may not be sold. She may be made a slave. One of the documents (a marriage contract) from Nuzi also says that if the wife is barren, she must provide another woman for her husband. When a child arrives as a result of the union, however, the wife cannot drive out the child, as Sarah drove out Ishmael (Genesis 21:10).[4]

NOTES

1. Howard P. Colson, *Preparing to Teach the Bible* (Nashville, Tennessee: Convention Press, 1959), 67.

2. For a fuller understanding of Bible translations, see the article in *Christianity Today* by Leslie R. Keylock entitled, "Bible Translations, A Guide through the Forest" (Volume 27, April 22, 1983, 10-15).

3. Olin T. Binkley, *How to Study the Bible*, (Nashville, Tennessee: Convention Press, 1969), 150-153.

4. Ibid., 154.

Chapter V

How to Prepare a Bible Lesson*

Everything we have said in the earlier chapters of this book must be consciously and unconsciously applied here. All teachers know that fruitful teaching results from wise planning. Your best Sunday school or midweek Bible study lessons have been those that you have planned well. How does one plan well?

First, teachers should begin by preparing themselves through prayer and meditation. Prayer helps to purify us and get us ready to be instruments in God's hands to bless others. Teachers should not only pray for themselves, but should pray also for the students. Pray that God will touch their hearts and minds to help prepare them for the reception of the truths that are to be shared on a given occasion.

After one has prayed and continues to pray, then he or she is ready to begin mastering the biblical material for the given occasion—whether it is a Sunday school lesson or a Bible lesson for a mid-week setting. If you are preparing to teach a Sunday school lesson, you should begin early in the week. Most experts in this area recommend that you begin reading the biblical material on Sunday afternoon and continue to meditate on it all during the week. Most Sunday schools have Home Daily Bible Readings printed in the lesson format. Where this is the case, one should read and meditate on each passage daily until they are well digested.

Most Sunday school lessons have a general subject. The Committee on the Uniform Series of Sunday School Lessons normally gives appropriate titles to each lesson, whether for adults or children. One

---

*This chapter focuses primarily on teaching adults.

should study, carefully, the subject to ascertain the essence of the lesson. Sometimes, this is called the central truth of the lesson. In a preaching context, Harry Emerson Fosdick called this the "big truth." The big truth always grows out of the printed text for the Sunday school lesson. After one has studied on the big truth of the lesson, one should then begin to gather material to help amplify, clarify, and illustrate the big truth or central point. You may begin with your denomination's Sunday school quarterly, as well as the annual Sunday school lesson commentaries. In these, you will find very helpful information. These quarterlies and commentaries usually contain the printed text, introduction to the lesson, the lesson text explained verse by verse or idea by idea, and a section on the lesson applied to our times. After one has read and digested these resource materials and made appropriate notes, he/she, then, may want to read about the printed text in other commentaries. (See section on commentaries in the chapter on "Tools and Aids for Bible Study.")

After you have finished the preceding assignments, you are then ready to outline, organize, and write your lesson in full manuscript form. At this point, you may want to use the outline in your favorite Sunday school commentary or you may want to develop your own. Either way, you definitely will need an outline to follow in order to wisely organize your thoughts. Even after you have written your lesson in a full manuscript form, it is better to teach it from a detailed outline form. This helps to give you better eye contact with your pupils and a freer spirit for fresh flashes or breezes from the Holy Spirit.

While praying, reading, and meditating for this teaching session, do it with the students' needs in mind, as well as the goals which you plan to accomplish in the lesson. And, of course, you want to tailor the material to fit your students' needs.

The Students' Needs

What are the students' needs in relation to the central truth of the lesson? In order to know the students' needs, you (the teacher) have to know your students. Thus, it is wise to interact with your students every chance you get so you can know—best—how to understand their growing edge and meet their needs. Regarding students' needs, Colson is on target as he quotes from Dobbins:

> In preparation for teaching, you need to study not only the Bible but your pupils as well—their problems and their needs—if you are to do your best work.
>
> Dr. Dobbins offers some good suggestions in what he calls "A Practical Program of Pupil Study." This plan calls for the teacher to have a notebook with a page for each pupil. On each page, with sufficient space between each heading, the following items should be listed: (1) Home life, (2) Community surroundings, (3) School life, (4) Work life, (5) Companionships, (6) Special interests and abilities, (7) Temperament and disposition, (8) Moral and spiritual difficulties, (9) Biblical and religious knowledge, and (10) Relationship to Christ and the church. Under each heading, Dr. Dobbins has a series of pertinent questions to guide a teacher in gathering the desired information.
>
> Findley B. Edge also finds a similar comprehensive list of questions in *Teaching for Results*. Naturally, it will take time to get all the facts needed about each pupil, but one should work persistently at the job. As your knowledge of each one grows, your effectiveness with each one will also grow.[1]

Furthermore, Colson declares this:

> Visitation is the best way to get to know your pupils. By calling on them in their homes, you will not only establish a closer contact with them, but will also gain valuable insights into their family situations. Teachers of children need to know the parents of those whom they teach. In the case of some adults, visits to their places of work may occasionally be advisable. But on the whole, the best place to do visitation is in the homes.[2]

Richard Rusbuldt's "Thirteen Steps in Planning a Session" is also helpful in identifying and responding to the students' needs, regardless of what age they are.[3] He gives the following practical information to help the teacher decide to actively respond toward identifying and meeting the students' needs and concerns. He places these concerns and responses in the following columns:

The Concern	Passive Concern	Active Response
Joe was laid off last week.	You know about it but you will ignore it in order not to embarrass Joe.	Express your concern to Joe. Pray for Joe and the family. Keep your ears open for job openings.
Susie (six years old) will have an operation this week. She's afraid.	Don't mention it because it will cause more fear and distrust. Pray for her privately.	Tell her you (or others from the class) will be in to see her. Pray for her in the class. Visit her.
Over half the class is coming late every Sunday.	Ignore it, or complain to the class. Make session plans accordingly.	Discuss it with the class. What are the reasons? Can anything be done about it? Check out expectations.

Rusbuldt reminds teachers that even though we may not always have the right words and answers for our students' needs, we should still exemplify care and concern:

> Even when you don't know what to say to your students, somehow let them know you care for them. The passive response only has meaning for you; the active response provides for the transfer of your feelings to the students.[4]

Also, one needs to use words, phrases, and illustrations which are applicable to the particular students you are teaching. A teacher in the Junior Department would not want to use sophisticated, theological terms like atonement, justification, sanctification, consecration, and the like. Rather, you would use terms which your students understand. (Oh, I am sure it is all right to teach them new word concepts from time to time, but we must always be careful that we communicate with them and not lose them.) Moreover, too often teachers use illustrations which are not understood by their students. The illustration in the lesson is like a window in your house—it should shed light on the subject. Jesus was a master at using illustrations which were applicable to His audience's needs. His parables are classic examples. He could tell parabolic stories which made His points in clear and cogent ways. Who could miss the point of the profound love and forgiveness of God in the *Parable of the Prodigal Son*? Who could miss the point of the need to cultivate diligence and faithfulness in one's God-given abilities and investments in the *Parable of the Talents*? Who could miss the point of who the neighbor was in the *Parable of the Good Samaritan*? Jesus communicated with people on their levels. We should do likewise. Good illustrations are all around us. We get them from daily observations, talking with friends and strangers, television,* reading commentaries, biographies (I love illustrations from people's life stories), newspapers, comic strips, novels, and the like. Whenever an illustration jolts you to the point that you say, "That will teach," then write it down and use it at the appropriate time. It is wise to file illustrations under headings and keep them for future use.

Clarify Your Teaching Goals

Now that you have prayed, studied, researched and gathered materials, and you are ready for your final organization of the lesson to be taught, it is wise to reclarify your goal. What is your goal for today's lesson?

What do you intend to accomplish? Do you intend for your students to be more loving? experience more joy in their lives? learn how to celebrate in worship? grow in kindness toward each other? cultivate discipleship? become more cooperative or grow in encouraging or helping one another? Of course, your big truth or central idea of the lesson will help guide you at this point. In refining your goals, you would want to ask, "What lesson(s) do I hope that each student will have learned when this class period is finished?" Thus, your teaching goals must be shaped accordingly!

---

*Some of my best illustrations in lessons and sermons have come to me while watching television commercials. For example, the Burger King commercial: "Have it your way"; the Wendy's commercial: "Where is the beef?" the Brylcreem commercial: "A little dab will do you," etc.

Developing a Lesson Plan

A good lesson plan is simply the clear and concise arrangement of the material and methods that a teacher plans to use in order to help students acquire and apply knowledge (biblical truths).

The basic components of a good lesson plan, according to the experts, are as follows:

- **Your aim or objective.** (Almost all Sunday school commentaries give one or more aims for each lesson.)
- **Materials.** (e.g., Bible, Sunday school commentary, filmstrips, pictures, maps, crayons, projector and screen, and the like.)
- **Your plan of presentation.** (This includes the introduction, your lesson outline, method of communicating the central truth of the lesson, activities, and the like.)
- **Evaluation.** (During and after each lesson, a teacher should seek to measure the effectiveness of the class session.)

Use of Methods in Teaching the Lesson

Guy P. Leavitt asserts that there are two basic and effective methods of teaching: one is by impression—that is, what one sees, hears, smells, feels, or tastes—use of the senses. The other is by expression—he thinks, speaks, or acts.[5] Of course, the wise teacher knows that these two methods overlap in the teaching and learning process.

Under the impression method of teaching, Leavitt lists the following methods.[6]

- Bible in Hand
- Bulletin Board
- Chalkboard
- Chart
- Display
- Film strips and Slides
- Flannelgraph
- Object Lesson
- Overhead Projector
- Prep-Box
- Pictures
- Puppets
- Reading
- Record Player or Tape Recorder

- Lecture
- Story or Illustration
- Map and Globe

Under the methods of expression, he lists the following with brief statements of explanation:[7]

ASSIGNMENT

What It Is: The assignment method consists of the teacher asking a pupil to prepare in advance for participation in the lesson. The method is best for teenagers and adults, but can be used in classes of middlers and juniors.

BUZZ SESSION

What It Is: A buzz group is a small group of three to seven people who buzz (talk) for a brief time about a problem assigned to them by the teacher. They arrive at a group conclusion that is then presented to the class as a whole. This is useful with youth and adults.

CHECK CHART

What It Is: A check chart is a questionnaire which may be answered by checking the answers to questions.

COLLAGE OR MONTAGE

What It Is: A montage is a series of pictures arranged in order to expand a theme. The pictures usually overlap each other so that no white space is left. A collage adds a three-dimensional effect to the pictures.

CONVERSATION

What It Is: the teacher and pupils talk about the lesson theme in a conversational manner, not as a discussion.

How to Use It: Conversation is used frequently for teaching children. The conversation usually occurs around a browsing table or in an interest center. The teacher leads in the conversation, often using a question to establish contact. For example, the teacher may say, "What do you have in your hand, Charlie?" From some such simple opening, the teacher proceeds to direct the talk in a way that contributes to the achievement of the lesson aim. Carefully avoid preaching or lecturing, but do try to get the pupil to become so interested that he will talk with you about the subject.

DEBATE

What It Is: Two teams participate—the affirmative and the negative. Each debater speaks briefly. After all have spoken, one member on each side has a few minutes for rebuttal to disprove the other team's claims and to reaffirm his own.

DISCUSSION

What It Is: Discussion is one of the most effective means of generating pupil participation. It may be used in classes with older children up through adults. One of its chief advantages is discovering and clarifying misconceptions. Discussion is also an effective way of determining just what each pupil needs to know to complete his understanding of a subject. It also encourages pupils to think.

DRAMA

What It Is: Drama may range from pantomiming a Bible story in a children's class to writing and producing a dramatization to apply a biblical truth in an older class. In either case, the pupil learns by acting out a part.

DRILL

What It Is: Drill is not merely memorization, although that is part of it, nor is it mere learning by rote or by rule. It is, instead, a learning process which furnishes automatic, recurring responses that will be helpful. Learning the books of the Bible in their proper order may be memorization, but it is also a means of helping the pupil to turn immediately to a desired Bible passage.

FINGERPLAYS

What It Is: The teacher tells a story to preschool children, using the fingers as characters in the story or parts of a scene. The children "play the story" with the teacher.

Action rhymes are related to fingerplays, but action is not limited to the fingers; the whole body can become involved. Action rhymes are helpful for young children who have not yet developed the use of small muscles.

HANDWORK

What It Is: Handwork includes creative activity done by the pupils, such as freehand drawing, coloring, dot-to-dot drawing, cutouts, stand-ups, patterns, posters, murals, sandtable fingers, finger painting, clay modeling, and similar activities. Although older pupils learn by making replicas, maps, posters, banners, and Bible pictures, handwork is limited almost entirely to the children's department.

MARCH OR RHYTHM

What It Is: Young children require activity. March or rhythm is a good way to actively involve the children in expressing the teaching of the lesson.

MUSIC

What It Is: Music may be used, in a variety of ways, to teach. Songs may be used to reinforce Bible concepts and facts. Older pupils may write new words, based on a Bible message, to existing music.

PANEL DISCUSSION

What It Is: Two or more members of the class, each fully informed and integrated to one phase of a subject, discuss the subject while the other pupils listen.

How to Use It: A panel discussion is best used in classes of teens or adults. The subject chosen should have as many phases as there are members of the panel. The participants are to do research work, have notes in hand, and be adequately prepared to bring out all of the lesson teachings possible.

PROBLEM

What It Is: In math, the young learner began with simple problems: "John had four apples. He gave one to Jim. How many did he have left?" As he advanced in school, the problems became more complicated. In daily living, he is called upon to solve all kinds of problems. In solving them, he learns. In the Sunday school class, the teacher uses the problem-solving technique to help the pupil to learn in the same way.

QUESTION

What It Is: A question reveals knowledge and provokes thinking. It is an inquiry—the act of asking. The teacher needs to know how to ask questions in a way that will stimulate and guide learning. He must also know how to answer questions in a way that will aid the pupil to learn. If the pupil does not think, he does not learn. Jesus made frequent use of the question method, and His answers to questions are invariably effective, generally leading to more thinking and often to action.

PROJECT

What It Is: A project is putting a lesson aim into practice. Suppose the purpose of the lesson is to encourage love for others. A child could try to help his or her mother by putting away toys after they are used. Juniors could run errands, shovel snow, mow lawns. Teens could visit shut-ins and conduct worship services or distribute gifts to the poor. Young adults could visit the inmates or patients of public institutions such as the jail, hospital, or nursing home. Adults could collect gifts of money for someone in need, buy eyeglasses for children and aged persons unable to afford them, paint a widow's house, or do a variety of other things.

REVIEW

What It Is: A test or review is necessary for the teacher's evaluation of his or her teaching and of the pupil's learning. It has other advantages, too, such as helping pupils to crystallize ideas, reinforce attitudes, revive interest, fix the lesson in memory, and make more of an effort to learn.

WORKBOOK

What It Is: The workbook contains questions and activities for the pupil to answer, and problems and puzzles for him or her to solve under the teacher's supervision during the class session. The contents are discussed either prior to the use of the workbook or afterward. Usually workbooks, often called pupil's books, are available from the publisher who prints the teacher's manual and other supplies for the lesson course.

A teacher must choose his or her method(s) according to the age levels and needs of his or her students. Most teachers will soon find the methods which best suit them and their class needs, and will stay with them week after week. In normal adult teaching situations, I have found that I lean heavily on the discussion/lecture method. However, that probably would not hold true for the smaller children's classes. Variety is good for all teachers, and we should occasionally experiment with an assortment of methods. Whatever method and lesson plan you use, you need to be sure that it facilitates your teaching goals and objectives.

In that light, a further word on evaluation needs to be said. The wise teacher continues to consciously evaluate himself or herself to see if he or she is being effective as a teacher of the Word of God. I find the following two evaluation instruments by Leavitt[8] very helpful for all who teach the Word of God:

Evaluating Lesson Presentation

	Yes	No	Don't Know

Lesson Aim

Did I have a teaching aim clearly in mind?

Did I make it clear to the pupils?

Did I keep it clearly understood throughout the lesson presentation?

Do I believe the aim was accomplished?

Beginning the Lesson

Did I start the lesson on time?

Did the opening catch the attention of every pupil?

Was the opening true to the teaching aim?

Was it appropriate?

Was it pleasing to the pupils?

As an opening method, would I say it was the best I could have used?

Main Points of Bible Study

Was each point clearly understood by all?

Were all the pupils interested?

Did I include one or more points that should have been omitted?

Did I overlook one or more points that should have been explained?

Did I give each point the amount of time it should have received?

Do I feel the Lord was pleased with the way I applied His holy Word?

Did I involve the pupils in the lesson?

Main Point of Application

Did each pupil understand how the teachings applied to his or her life?

Do I believe each pupil will do as taught?

Did I include one or more applications that should have been omitted?

Did I overlook one or more applications that should have been included?

Did I give each application the emphasis it should have had?

Do I feel the Lord was pleased with the way I applied His teachings?

Closing the Lesson

Did I close the lesson when I should have?

Did the closing emphasize the teaching aim?

Did I finish all I had planned to say and do in presenting the lesson?

Would the pupils have enjoyed a longer lesson period?

Was the method of closing the best I could have used?

Do I believe every pupil will want to come back next Sunday because he or she believes my lessons are worth the effort?

My Job and I

To check your qualifications and your success in your job in the church's Sunday morning Bible school, put an "X" in the "yes" or "no" column, or put a number from 1 to 4 in the "partly" column after each question. Then multiply the number of "yes" marks by 5, add the number in the "partly" column, and you have your grade.

A. I Am a Worker for the Lord

Yes	No	Partly

1. As a Christian, I am a worker for the Lord. Am I doing the work for which I am best fitted?

B. My Evaluation of My Spiritual Qualifications

2. Am I thoroughly committed to the Christian work entrusted to me, willing to make the sacrifices necessary for success?

3. Am I an active, supporting member of my local church?

4. In my home life, am I a Christian as shown in my relationship with the members of my family, my daily reading of God's Word, meditation, and prayer?

5. In public, are my dress, words, actions, and general behavior such as to bring honor to my Lord?

C. My Evaluation of My Improvement in My Job

6. Have I taken the elemental training courses pertaining to my work in the church Sunday school?

7. Am I continuing to improve myself as a worker by further training?

	Yes	No	Don't Know

8. Do I own and use a personal library pertaining to my work?

9. Do I practice self-development through individual reading and study?

10. Do I practice self-development through observation, visiting other schools, attending laboratory classes, and demonstrations?

D. My Evaluation of My Ability as a Leader

	Yes	No	Don't Know

11. Do I make the best use possible of suggestions from the head of my department in the Sunday school?

12. Am I on friendly and cooperative terms with the other workers in my church and its Sunday school?

13. Am I reliable, dependable, and trustworthy?

14. Am I constantly on the lookout to discover and help train new workers in the church and its school?

15. Are my motives in my work above criticism?

E. My Evaluation of My Efforts

16. Do I devote at least one hour to my work each week, not counting Sunday or the time given to preparation for Sunday?

17. Am I always fully prepared for my work on Sunday morning?

	Yes	No	Don't Know

18. Am I present at least fifteen minutes early on Sunday morning?

19. Do I make it a rule to begin and to stop exactly on time in my Sunday morning session?

20. Am I satisfied that I am doing my best in the work for which I have been selected?

Total

My Grade is

Leavitt[9] also gives an interesting and helpful STUDENT'S BIBLE SCHOOL CLASS AND TEACHER EVALUATION instrument:

Student's Bible School Class and Teacher Evaluation

Please underline what you consider to be the most accurate words or phrases within the parentheses in each of the statements below. For the good of your class and teacher, please be perfectly honest. We are seeking to find the areas in which our Bible school can be improved. Your honest opinion will help. Please do not sign this paper or in any way identify yourself. Thanks!

1. I (have, have not) noted improvement in my teacher's teaching in the past six months.

2. My teacher's preparation (always, usually, seldom, never) seems quite adequate.

3. My teacher (does, does not) invite class discussion and (does, does not) allow enough opportunity for it.

4. My teacher (does, does not) emphasize the connection between lessons in a series from Sunday to Sunday.

5. My teacher (does, does not) usually hold my interest and attention through a whole lesson period.

6. My teacher (does, does not) seem genuinely glad to see me each Sunday morning.

7. I (always, usually, seldom, never) learn something worthwhile from my teacher's presentation of the Bible school lesson.
8. My teacher's teaching method (does, does not) stir me to independent thought on the subject or lesson being taught.
9. I (think, do not think) that a more active class social program would be beneficial to my class.
10. If for any reason I am forced to miss a Bible school lesson, I (would, would not) feel that I had missed very much.
11. The activities of my class and the skills of my teacher are such that I (am, am not) always proud to invite my friends to come to Bible school with me.
12. I think the time allotted for lesson study, if properly used, (is, is not) long enough.
13. Offhand, I (could, could not) tell anyone the main points in last Sunday's lesson.
14. My teacher (has, has not) made a call to my home within the last year.

A Sample Lesson with Analyses
(THE TEACHER'S QUARTERLY)

Lesson Unit: **A Study of the Major Prophets**
Adult Topic: **An Extraordinary Vision of God**
Background Scripture: *Isaiah 6*
Printed Text: *Isaiah 6:1-8*

King James Version	*Revised Standard Version*
IN THE year that king Uzziah died I saw also the LORD sitting upon a throne, high and lifted up, and his train filled the temple.	IN THE year that King Uzziah died I saw the Lord sitting upon a throne, high and lifted up; and his train filled the temple.
2 Above it stood the seraphims: each one had six wings; with twain he covered his face, and with twain he covered his feet, and with twain he did fly.	2 Above him stood the seraphim; each had six wings; with two he covered his face, and with two he covered his feet, and with two he flew.
3 And one cried unto another, and said, Holy, holy, holy, is the LORD of hosts: the whole earth is full of his glory.	3 And one called to another and said: "Holy, holy, holy is the LORD of hosts; the whole earth is full of his glory."
4 And the posts of the door moved at the voice of him that cried, and the house was filled with smoke.	4 And the foundations of the thresholds shook at the voice of him who called, and the house was filled with smoke.
5 Then said I, Woe is me! For I am undone; because I am a man of unclean lips, and I dwell in the midst of a people of unclean lips: for mine eyes have seen the King, the LORD of hosts.	5 And I said: "Woe is me! For I am lost; for I am a man of unclean lips, and I dwell in the midst of a people of unclean lips; for my eyes have seen the King, the LORD of hosts!"
6 Then flew one of the seraphims unto me, having a live coal in his hand, which he had taken with the tongs from off the altar:	6 Then flew one of the seraphim to me, having in his hand a burning coal which he had taken with tongs from the altar.
7 And he laid it upon my mouth, and said, Lo, this hath touched thy lips; and thine iniquity is taken away, and thy sin purged.	7 And he touched my mouth, and said: "Behold, this has touched your lips; your guilt is taken away, and your sin forgiven."
8 Also I heard the voice of the Lord, saying, Whom shall I send, and who will go for us? Then said I, Here am I; send me.	8 And I heard the voice of the Lord saying, "Whom shall I send, and who will go for us?" Then I said, "Here am I! Send me."

Memory Verse: "Also I heard the voice of the Lord, saying, Whom shall I send, and who will go for us? Then said I, Here am I; send me" (KJV).

Home Daily Bible Readings
Monday—Isaiah 6
Tuesday—Jeremiah 1:1-15
Wednesday—Chronicles 26
Thursday—Ezekiel 1
Friday—Acts 9:1-2
Saturday—John 3:1-17
Sunday—John 9:35-41

LESSON OUTLINE

I. The Prophet's Extraordinary Vision of God (verses 1-3)

II. The Prophet's Vision Was Clear and Precise (verse 1b)

III. The Prophet Saw Himself in the Mirror of God's Holiness (verse 5)

IV. The Prophet Was Touched, Forgiven, and Commissioned by God (verses 6-8)

LESSON PURPOSE

To show how Isaiah's vision of God shaped, molded, and empowered his life for prophetic ministry. Likewise, it can give inspiration and insight to us to the extent that our vision of God can continuously break us, melt us, mold us, and empower us for fruitful and faithful Christian service.

INTRODUCTION

When a country is losing its moral grip and limping "hither, thither, and yon" politically, what do you think can help and cure it? When a church family is bickering and feuding over how to build the new church structure, or how to spend the church's budget, or members are arguing about who is the best candidate to support in a national political race, what do you think would be helpful and healing in this situation?

When a denominational group is caught in the throes of controversy over how to treat homosexuals, how to handle the issues of women in the preaching ministry, or how to prioritize its mission budget, what word is helpful here?

When people are drifting to and fro with no clear sense of what is important in life, what prescription would you offer for them?

Today's lesson, based on Isaiah's vision of God, can shed some biblical light on each one of these situations. It can help each person to see more clearly that God can and will provide, for us, fresh visions to guide our pathways week after week, and year after year.

LESSON BACKGROUND

Isaiah was born in Jerusalem about 760 BC, during the preaching period of his contemporary, Amos, who went north to Bethel to cry, "Let justice roll down like waters and righteousness like an everflowing stream." His prophetic ministry began about 740 BC, in the year that King Uzziah died. For the next forty years, he prophesied in Jerusalem, sharing with kings, princes, and average citizens the urgent message of the awesome God Jehovah.

Although he was probably influenced by the ministries of Hosea and Amos, his greatest influence came when he met God in the transforming and never-to-be-forgotten temple experience. In fact, God's holiness was so powerful and penetrating that when he later talked descriptively of God, he fondly referred to Him as the Holy One of Israel. Today's printed text constitutes this marvelous vision which Isaiah had of God.

THE LESSON, EXPLAINED AND APPLIED
I. The Prophet's Extraordinary Vision of God (verses 1-3)

One of the greatest needs of an individual, a church, a convention, a denomination, or a nation is to have and maintain a fresh and genuine vision of God. For, our visions of God will help shape our theology and our conduct, our doctrine and our duties, our orthodoxy and our orthopraxy.

First, our printed text reveals to us the moving and transforming vision that the young Isaiah had of God. He says, "In the year that King Uzziah died I saw the Lord sitting upon a throne, high and lifted up; and his train filled the temple" (Isaiah 6:1, RSV).

Very often, crises and circumstances in our lives help determine our levels of need for God. So is the case with Isaiah. King Uzziah's death shook Isaiah's life at its foundation. He was overwhelmed with grief and engulfed in despair. His world seemed as though it was about to crumble. His life felt like it was about to come unglued at the center. Overwhelmed with grief and laden with despondency, he apparently journeyed to the temple to talk with God. His conversation probably took this shape: "God, I am deeply saddened and grieved by the death of beloved King Uzziah. Lord, what will we do now that he is dead? How will we make it? What will happen to our beloved nation? Who will now take the helm of our national ship and lead us onward and upward? Who will become our new King and occupy the vacated throne of Uzziah?" But instead of God answering Isaiah in terms of an earthly throne, a replacement for King Uzziah, he lifted Isaiah up in the spirit, up beyond Jerusalem and Uzziah's empty throne, to the throne room in heaven and there Isaiah saw God on His throne high and lifted up... and His train filled the temple.

God did not really answer Isaiah's concerns about a replacement for Uzziah, but rather gave him a higher and more permanent answer. He was saying, "Isaiah, don't worry about Uzziah's throne being vacant, just be sure that you know mine is occupied. Isaiah, Uzziah can live and die and nothing extraordinary will shake the Earth; but, were my throne to be vacant, the whole Earth would take a dive into cosmic disintegration. Isaiah, Uzziah is dead but I am alive. I am on My throne, and as long as I am on My throne, I can help you handle your burdens and problems in Jerusalem."

So in Isaiah's vision from God, he was able to understand that when there was trouble and despair in Jerusalem, there was help from above. Someone has remarked that whenever there is trouble down here, there is help "up there." And so, we can affirm with Isaiah that in our downsitting and uprising, in our joys and our sorrows, in our tough times and our times of ease, in our ups and our downs, God can empower us with a fresh vision of Himself and reenergize us for continuous ministry. Thus, in the year that King Uzziah died, Isaiah had an overwhelming vision of God.

II. The Prophet's Vision Was Clear and Precise (verse 1b)

Second, Isaiah's vision of God was clear and precise. Let us observe that if one is going to represent God, that person needs to clarify his or her vision. He said that he saw God high and lifted up; and that the seraphim (angels) were surrounding the throne singing, "Holy, holy, holy is the LORD of hosts, the whole earth is full of his glory..." (Isaiah 6:3). Isaiah was clear and sure about what and whom he saw. Many people today see God, so they say; but their vision of Him is hazy, cloudy, and blurred. A few years ago, a young man said that God told him to go to Atlanta and kill Dr. Martin Luther King Sr. Thus, he journeyed to Atlanta and instead killed Mrs. King Sr. Certainly, that was an ungodly and senseless vision. But I press the point because the young man declared that God told him to kill. While that may be an absurd example, it makes my point: too many people have blurred and hazy visions of God which are not visions at all. Everybody who moves out for God is not necessarily equipped and armed with His vision.

The late Dr. Kelly Miller Smith Sr. of Nashville, Tennessee, told a story many years ago about a white man who came to visit his church when he lived in Mound Bayou, Mississippi. At the end of a worship service, after the choir had sung, the white man wanted to make some remarks. (In the old days, persons often made comments at the end of the worship concerning their feelings about the worship service.) When he stood, he said to the black congregation, "Oh, how I love to hear you all sing! You all sing so well. In fact, I love your singing so much that when I get to heaven, I am going to come over in you all's department and listen to you all sing." This man's vision of God was so blurred and hazy and out of tune with heaven's that he had reduced God to his own mentality of Mississippi segregation, and had God acting in heaven the same way that white people were acting in Mississippi. He had God compartmentalizing heaven with blacks on one side and whites on the other. What a cloudy and blurred vision of God!

Even as I write these words, many people still have unfocused visions of God. They are trying to reduce God to their size and their conceptions of Him. One way to avoid making this mistake is to take Martin Luther's advice. Martin Luther once said, "The spirit must be bound to the Word." That is, the vision that you receive from the Lord must always harmonize with the revelation of God in Jesus Christ. If your vision does not meet that standard, then you can be assured that it is not from God.

Isaiah's vision, however, was from God and was clear and basically precise. He saw God in His transcendence (high and lifted up) and in His immanence (His train filled the temple). Isaiah's vision of God is true to His self-disclosure on two levels: His "farness" and "nearness," His "upness" and "downness," His "transcendence" and His "immanence." For, indeed, God is high and holy, so holy that the heavenly creatures are pictured as having to cover their faces with their wings to protect them from His awesome, consuming presence and glory. God is indeed high above us in perfection, goodness, love, mercy, grace, and justice. But even though He is high above us, He has decided to come among us. The high God of the cosmos comes to the lowly creatures who are earthbound. That is what Isaiah means when he says, "His train filled the temple." In Isaiah's day, kings wore long robes that often had trains attached to them. Many of us saw the wedding of Prince Charles and Lady Diana some years ago. You probably noticed the beautiful wedding gown that Lady Diana wore, with its long, beautiful train. Now when Isaiah envisioned God, Isaiah said that the train on God's robe reached all the way down into the Jerusalem Temple; i.e., His train filled the temple. God's presence was represented on Earth by His train. God came to see about Isaiah in the temple, to minister to him. He came to bless his life, to transform and liberate him for ministry.

Today, we need this temple vision of God who is high and holy and whose train also fills our temples. We need a God above us who cannot be manipulated by us and who always comes to us to help us be our best selves. We need His train filling our earthly temples. We need His train filling temples in Washington, D.C. We need His presence filling state government houses. We need His presence filling local government seats. We need His presence in every home and every heart and life across America and the world. Thank God that in Jesus Christ it is now possible for His train most perfectly to fill God's world and our lives.

III. The Prophet Saw Himself in the Mirror of God's Holiness (verse 5)

Third, when Isaiah saw God, His righteousness became a mirror in which Isaiah saw himself and he cried, "Woe is me, for I am undone…" (Isaiah 6:5a). If one is serious about representing God, the person needs to allow such a vision of the Almighty to give him or her a clear picture of himself or herself. Whenever people get a true vision of God, they also get a true vision of self. They see that God is all-perfect, all-holy, all-wise, all-powerful, and ever-present. People understand that in the presence of God, they are sinful and unholy. No person can ever really meet God and not see himself or herself. When Job really met God, he declared from a prostrate posture, "I had heard of thee by the hearing of the ear, but now my eye sees thee; therefore I despise myself, and repent in dust and ashes" (Job 42:5-6, RSV). When Peter really saw the power of the Lord Jesus Christ, he ceased bragging about his strength and admitted his weakness: "Depart from me; for I am a sinful man, O Lord" (Luke 5:8b, KJV). All the saints through the ages have felt a keen sense of sin and contriteness in the presence of the almighty God. So it was in Isaiah's case that he saw and felt his burden of sin in the mirror of God's righteousness and cried, "Woe is me."

IV. The Prophet Was Touched, Forgiven, and Commissioned by God (verses 6-8)

Finally, when Isaiah made his confession to God, the Lord instructed the angel to go over to the altar and pick up a live coal of fire and touch the prophet's lips and tell him that his sins were forgiven and his iniquity was purged. God's holy presence, through His angel, was transforming, liberating Isaiah's soul from the shackles of sin and shame. Whenever one sees himself in the mirror of God's righteousness and becomes repentant before the Lord, he will be divinely touched, healed, and commissioned. One poet put it this way:

> Then the hand of Jesus touched me,
> And now I am no longer the same. ...
> He touched me and made me whole.

(The song "He Touched Me," by Bill and Gloria Gaither.)

After Isaiah was touched and made whole, he heard God saying, "Whom shall I send and who will go for us?" It was then that Isaiah answered, "Here am I, send me" (verse 8). Isaiah was now ready and equipped to be a prophetic missionary for God. His heart, his mind, and his body were now geared for preaching and teaching and spreading the message of God.

Did he represent God? Indeed he did! He went all over Judah telling people about what happened to him in the temple and sharing God's message with kings and commoners. He was able to inspire literally thousands and lead them to a high and noble road of life. He was able to help direct the national and international affairs of his day because he had been touched, saved, and commissioned by God. He, along with Amos, Hosea, and Micah, moved across the land of Judah with an awesome impact for good, nationally and individually. They literally turned the world upside down for God during the eighth century of Israel's history.

What about you and me? Are we serious about hearing God's call and answering it affirmatively? Will we share our vision of God? Are we serious about implementing God's agenda?

We should allow God's Holy Spirit to help us make up our minds to run for God. We should share His holy and liberating Word with people everywhere, because we know that He has power to save us and make us whole. Where there is injustice, let us shout, "Let justice roll down like waters, and righteousness like an everflowing stream" (Amos 5:24, RSV). Where His will is unclear, we should ask, "What doth the LORD require of thee, but to do justly, and to love mercy, and to walk humbly with thy God?" (Micah 6:8b, KJV). Where people are in doubt about His love, we should cry, "Look to Calvary; it is the highest expression of God's redemptive love." "For God so loved the world that he gave his only Son, that whoever believes in Him should not perish but have eternal life" (John 3:16, RSV).

We thank God for Isaiah, who, many years ago, went down to the temple burdened and despondent, and who was able to see God and find new insight and new vision for his life. That vision became the stimulation and inspiration for him to shout it out to the rest of the world that God is with us to redeem us, to love us, to liberate us, and to make us into the image of His own Son, Jesus. Oh what a mighty God we worship!

DISCUSSION QUESTIONS ON THE LESSON

1. With whose death is Isaiah's vision of God associated?
2. What impact did the king's death have on Isaiah and the nation of Judah?
3. What is your understanding of a vision from God?
4. Do all Christians have visions of God? Are they all clear, correct, and biblical?
5. How can you help to clarify a cloudy and hazy vision that someone has of God?
6. How did Isaiah's vision of God impact his life and ministry?
7. How has your vision of God influenced and impacted your life and ministry?
8. As a result of your vision of God, for what ministry have you been equipped?

AN ANALYSIS OF THE LESSON

The lesson topic was "An Extraordinary Vision of God." It was the second lesson in a quarter that dealt with the general theme, "A Study of the Major Prophets." This lesson, of course, was taught to an adult class. The teacher should always be aware of the relationship of the particular lesson on a given Sunday to the unit or quarterly theme. Here we sought to make that connection in the "Lesson Background."

Opening the Class. The teacher should always open the class with prayer, whether led by the teacher or a student. In this particular lesson, after the printed text has been read, the teacher should proceed with the background and introduction. Four illustrations were given in the introduction that can be used for discussion purposes during the course of the lesson's application. Introductions should not be too long—maybe four (4) to eight (8) minutes. An introduction to a lesson is like a porch on a house: it is only an entrance to the house, not the house.

Body of the Lesson. From the outline, you noticed that there were four main points lifted from the printed text. Each point was grounded in a particular verse(s). Then an exegesis and explanation were given on each verse. After the explanation of the meaning of the verse in context, then came the application. I prefer a lesson written with interpretation and application interwoven because it makes it easier if the teacher chooses to follow the printed lesson outline. Many Sunday school quarterlies give the interpretation of the text verse-by-verse in one section and then give the application at the end of the lesson. I prefer them running concurrently—interwoven. You probably noticed that the author intentionally captioned this section: "The Lesson Explained and Applied."

After the text was explained in light of Isaiah's day, you probably noticed that several illustrations were given to show how it can be applied to our day. I left open the illustrations in the introduction to be used imaginatively by the teacher.

There are study questions at the end of the lesson for the teacher to use as he or she sees best. They may be used at the end of the lesson, or they may be used in some other creative way.

Closing the Lesson. The teacher can probably close this lesson best with a summary and a brief statement of application and challenge.

Materials. Probably the only materials a teacher would need for the lesson would be a Bible, a Sunday school commentary, a map, and a chalkboard.

Method. The best method for teaching this lesson probably would be lecture/discussion, with a question here or there to encourage and excite participation. Of course, one would want to use the chalkboard to leave vivid impressions of the outline and demonstrative illustrations.

NOTES

1. Howard P. Colson, *Preparing to Teach the Bible* (Nashville, Tennessee: Convention Press, 1959), 104.

2. Ibid., 105.

3. Richard E. Rusbuldt, *Basic Teacher Skills* (Valley Forge, Pennsylvania: Judson Press, 1985), 54.

4. Ibid., 55.

5. Guy P. Leavitt, *Teach with Success* (Cincinnati, Ohio: Standard Publishing Company, Revised edition, 1989), 79.

6. Ibid., 81ff.

7. Ibid., see 100-109.

8. Ibid., 130, 138.

9. Ibid., 134.

Chapter VI

The Students We Teach*
(Twos through Teens)

In the previous chapter, the primary focus was on teaching adults. In this chapter, the focus will be on teaching children and youth, ages two through seventeen.

In the medical field, there is a state-of-the-art diagnostic device called a Magnetic Resonance Imaging machine, or an MRI machine. This machine is a highly complex piece of equipment. It is more sophisticated than the X-ray machine. The MRI takes three-dimensional pictures instead of the two-dimensional pictures that the X-ray machine takes. It is able to show images in three dimensions: frontal-view, side-view, and inner-view.

As teachers, it is important that you know your students from a "three-dimensional" perspective: Physio-social, mental, and emotional. It is hoped that this "Three-D" approach will assist you in providing the best learning opportunities for your students. This chapter is by no means a thorough study of these age groups. Rather, it is quite suggestive at best.

Dorothy Jean Furnish[1], in her book, *Experiencing the Bible with Children*, reminds us that children and youth with whom we come into contact, and whom we teach, live in a much different world than the one in which you or I grew up. She states that children and youth today are confronted by a series of issues that were minimal to non-existent for us. Several of the issues that she mentions focus on the future, the family structure, the

---

*This chapter is written in collaboration with Michelle Cobb, M.C.E., M.Div., former Director of Christian Education at First Baptist Church, Huntsville, Alabama. She holds a pastorate in Gary, Indiana.

educational system, violence, societal changes, and information gathering. Children and youth today, Furnish believes, do not have a clear understanding of what their future will be. It is somewhat unpredictable. She says this:

> "The unpredictability of the future may be one of the most significant ways in which our world differs from other times. Margaret Mead points out that a few generations ago, children could visualize their future adulthood by watching their grandparents. Now parents and grandparents find their own lifestyles influenced by the lifestyles of the young. The continuity between past and future seems to be broken, resulting in an uncertain present and an unpredictable future."[2]

The instability of the family structure is another issue of concern for children and youth. The stability that was provided by the two-parent home is being shaken by the single-parent home and the high divorce rate. The stability that was provided by the extended family is also shaken and threatened. Children and youth today are finding themselves confronted by family models—for example, adult homosexuals, non-married adults, communal living, etc.—which do not reflect Judeo-Christian teachings.

The educational system is another area of concern for youth, especially. The relevancy of the materials studied for the next century has been brought into question. This question is also being raised by the institutions of higher education and the business community as well, according to Furnish.

Furnish reminds us that violence in our society has an influence on children and youth, directly and indirectly. There are children who can recount, word for word, the horror of wars that they have viewed on television. There are youth who have experienced, firsthand, the death of a loved one due to gangs and/or guns. The movie *Boyz in the Hood* is a good case in point.

Societal changes affect children and youth of today as well. We live in a pluralistic society. The awareness of and appreciation for African-American, Native-American, Hispanic, and Asian-American cultures is evidenced as we examine the emphases that these ethnic groups are receiving. Our society is no longer seen as a White American society. The Christian teacher must therefore be sensitive to these changes as he or she teaches in this pluralistic society.

Finally, Furnish asserts that because we are living in a time when a great amount of knowledge is available (knowledge explosion), it is important that children and youth today learn the best and most up-to-date techniques for gathering and storing information. She states that "The ability to retrieve information from libraries and computers will be even more important."[4]

Now that a brief sketch has been given of the student's world, let us turn our attention to the specific age groups that we teach.

TWOS AND THREES

General Traits and Characteristics

The twos and threes are very active, physically. One of my friends refers to them as the "terrible twos." They tire easily; therefore, there is a need to provide a rest period after a very active period. Play is "work" to the children in these age groups. They take their play very seriously. Children two years of age do not play "with" other children, but engage in what is called "parallel" play. In other words, children may be in close range to other children, but they are in their own "play" worlds. This age group has very short attention spans and is very curious. Three-year-olds play with other children, preferably in small groups.[5]

Emotionally, the children in these age groups are in need of love. That need may sometimes be demonstrated by unacceptable behavior. Teachers will also observe that the students need to be the center of attention. It is difficult for this age group to share you with others. You will also observe your students attempting to be independent. This is sometimes demonstrated by their attempt to carry out certain tasks by themselves.[6]

Implications for Spiritual Development

Because of these students' need for love, they will better understand the concept, "God loves you," if they experience love from the teacher and other trusting adults. They will be able to identify with the concept that Jesus has a special concern for children because they witness your concern for them. The students in these two age groups can understand that the Bible is a significant book for adults. Finally, children in these age groups can identify with the church if others in the church help to make them feel that they are a part of the church.[7]

Suggested Teaching Methods and Activities

Create a stable environment. Use consistent discipline. Tell simple Bible stories using short sentences. Sing simple songs. Utilize simple puzzles. Emphasize Jesus as a special friend and the Bible as a special book. Use picture cards and puppets.

FOURS AND FIVES

General Traits and Characteristics

The world of fours and fives is a busy one. Children in these age groups are more independent, more curious, more vocal, and more active than the twos and threes. Because of the increased activity level, it is necessary to offset busy activities with quiet activities. Quiet activities may be extended because of the age levels.

Fours and fives enjoy playing with other children. However, they do prefer the attention of the teacher. The children in these age groups share their toys and possessions more readily than the twos and threes.

The imaginations of fours and fives are keen and provide for the creation of activities by the children in these age groups. These students' abilities to verbalize are greatly increasing because of their greater command of the spoken language. The students in these age groups are able to identify with the feelings of others. Increasingly, these students are able to make decisions and they should be encouraged to do so.

Implications for Spiritual Development

Through trusting and loving adults, fours and fives are able to understand that God loves and cares for them.[8] Fours and fives are also able to comprehend, through the behavior of trusting and loving adults, that Jesus is a loving person. Acceptance, and to a limited degree the need to forgive and to be forgiven, are concepts that the fours and fives are able to grasp.

The church is viewed as a special place, and the Bible is also seen as a book that is special. Fours and fives are able to pray very easily, and should be encouraged to do so.[9] From the spiritual perspective, the students in these age groups believe what they are told. You must be careful to relay true facts to them.[10]

Suggested Teaching Methods and Activities

Maintain a stable environment. Use consistent discipline. Teachers must be loving. Change activities frequently. Use drama, guided play, fingerplays, music, puzzles, art activities, stories, pictures, puppets, bulletin boards, and object lessons.

SIXES AND SEVENS

General Traits and Characteristics

The six- and seven-year-olds have a great amount of energy. It is very difficult for them to sit still for a long time. Their small muscles are developing, and their eye-hand coordination is improving. The abilities of six- and seven-year-olds are also improving in the areas of math, reading, and writing. Because of their ability to think only in concrete terms and not abstractly, they have a poor sense of the concept of time. Their listening vocabulary is greater than their speaking or reading vocabulary. Attention span is about 7-15 minutes.

These students are becoming more aware of the needs of those around them. They are developing a sense of morality: an understanding of right and wrong. The children in these age groups have a need to be praised by others and to belong. They need to feel wanted. Sometimes, they may appear to be bossy.

Your students will attempt to follow the rules. They desire and attempt to do well, although they often fail. Many of your students will not be embarrassed to show affection.[11] Students are able to understand the concept of a loving God by experiencing love from significant others in their lives, such as yourself. Because your students are able to think only in concrete terms (what they can see) and not in abstract terms (what they cannot see), they will have difficulty making the transition from the literal to the symbolic.[12]

Suggested Methods and Teaching Activities

The teacher should use the methods of storytelling, Bible games, music, art activities, puppets, reading, memorization, drama, and the like.

EIGHTS AND NINES

General Traits and Characteristics

Students in these age groups are able to work at tasks for longer periods of time. Because of the development of their fine motor skills, they are able to complete a better quality of work. The issues of "rightness" and "wrongness" are of concern to your students. They lean toward perfection, and many times set unrealistic goals for themselves.

The students' relationships with their peers are very important. They still enjoy adult assistance at times, although increasingly they enjoy being self-sufficient. Students in these age groups are in need of positive adult role models. The students in these age groups also identify with heroes and become involved with worshipping them.

Implications for Spiritual Development

Your students will grow in their faith by observing adults, such as you, live out their faith. Because your students think concretely and not abstractly, it is necessary for you to guide them in their understanding of how biblical truths apply to their lives. Your students are able to comprehend God as a "real" Being with whom they can share anything. God is also viewed as the "Creator."

Jesus is viewed by the students in these age groups as a special person because of His intimate relationship with God. Jesus is viewed as the primary instructor to teach how God desires people to live. These students understand Jesus as Savior; they are beginning to conceptualize sin and the need for salvation. They understand the church as "the people of God."

These students are able to participate in the life of the church at the level that their actions can reflect the teachings of Jesus.[13]

Suggested Teaching Methods and Activities

The teacher may use role-playing, puppets, Bible games, Bible stories, Bible research, art activities, music, memorizing Bible verses/books of the Bible/special Bible passages (Psalm 23, etc.), drama, and how to use your Bible.

TENS THROUGH TWELVES

General Traits and Characteristics

There are unique characteristics between the sexes in the ten-through-twelve-year-old age groups. The female students are developing physically at a much faster pace than the male students. These growth spurts make your students tire easily, a sign that is sometimes read as "laziness" by adults. Socially, the two sexes are beginning to form their unique sexuality identification. Not surprisingly, the peer group takes on significant importance.

Emotionally, your students have a need to be accepted by their peers. They also are looking for heroes to adopt, whether from fiction or real life. Your students are competitive, moody, and self-conscious.

Students in this age group are beginning to think in abstract terms. Their concentration is increasing, and their ability to understand history and the significance and meaning of events is increasing because of their newfound ability. Finally, your students enjoy planning and carrying out original ideas, because their interests, talents, and skills are developing.

Implication for Spiritual Development

Your students have the capability to relate to God in a very personal way, because they are able to know what God is like through Jesus. They are able to act out, in their lives, what they believe about Jesus and His teaching. For some of your students, Jesus takes on the role of a hero. It is wise to teach this age group about other biblical characters and extra-biblical characters who may become, for them, positive role models. Your students are able to grasp several theological concepts: God as Creator can be depended upon, and expects humankind to care for creation; and that God speaks in many ways—through Jesus, the Bible, other people, and creation.

Some of your students may express questions that they have about God. Others may commit themselves to Jesus Christ and unite with His church. The church, for these students, is the community of faith. The church also is where they need to hear Bible stories that relate to their everyday experiences.[14]

Suggested Teaching Methods and Activities

The teacher may use memory work, art, music, role-playing, Bible research, field trips, puppets, reading, listening, readings from the Bible, projects, a map and globe, filmstrips and slides, an overhead projector, and review.

TEENAGERS (Thirteen through Seventeen)

I believe it is wise for us to look more carefully and fully at the age group that we call teens and adolescents. We should give more attention to this age group because great changes are taking place in their lives. They are particularly experiencing physical and emotional changes. This maturation of body and emotions is often called puberty. Social scientists remind us that during this period, the students are changing in height, weight, body build, voice, facial appearance, and the like. I remember as a boy that I was shocked immensely with how fast one's body can change during this period of growth and development. One of my best friends and I were about the same height when school was out in May. When we returned to school in early September, I was shocked to see that he was almost two inches taller than I was and had taken on about 10-15 extra pounds in weight. Also during this period, many teens develop acne and other facial problems—some more pronounced than others. Because of all these changes, some teens become self-conscious. They notice the changes and are aware that other people are also noticing these changes. At points, some become too concerned and preoccupied with these changes, and some even become frightened and develop guilt feelings, asserts Annie Byrd, because they do not realize that the puberty period is normal, desirable, and God-intended.[15]

Implications for Spiritual Development

When teens face the problems and pressures of puberty, it is the job of the Sunday school and Bible class teachers to help them to understand and appreciate these changes by putting them in biblical and theological perspectives. Church teachers should join with the home in helping these youngsters to understand that the hand and mind of our wonderful and infinite God have made them, and that these changes are normal processes of human growth and development. As a part of the student's larger environment, teachers should always help facilitate and not complicate this normal process of maturation.

Not only are adolescents faced with bodily and emotional changes, but their analytical faculties are awakening, and they are beginning to explore and ask new questions about themselves and their world: Who am I? Why was I born? What do my peers and friends think of me? What do I think of myself? Do my parents really love me? Am I pretty/handsome or ugly? How do I fit in this huge world? What am I going to do with my life? What career should I choose? These and many other questions emerge in the minds of teenagers.

Much of what was said in the preceding paragraph has to do with teenagers developing proper and healthy concepts of themselves. It involves that all-important word called self-esteem. How a teenager answers the above questions will depend on his or her development of sound self-esteem. Also, a teenager's self-esteem is in direct relationship with how he or she esteems God. When one does not love himself or herself properly and in a healthy way, one has real difficulty loving others, including God.

The issue, then, is this: how can Christian teachers help these adolescents cope with all these questions and concerns? First, teachers should help to lead the teenager to understand the "conversion experience." If the teenager has not given his or her life to Jesus, it is the job of the teacher to help the student understand the need for an experience of forgiveness and wholeness that only comes through the saving grace of God in Jesus Christ, as the student commits his or her life to Christ. If the teenager is already converted, it is the job of the teacher to facilitate the "growing in grace" process. That growing in grace process, or course, is strengthened and guided by the teenager's church membership and discipleship experiences. Each teacher should help students to understand that the New Testament requires us to grow in (1) prayer; (2) Bible study; (3) worship (both private and public); (4) giving of time, talents, and money; and (5) Christian attitudes and appreciations. Under the caption of "Christian Attitudes and Appreciations," Byrd asserts that pupils should develop attitudes and appreciations in every area of their experience. She lists five areas:

> (1) **Regarding God**—As the teenager develops in his concept of God, his love for the heavenly Father and Jesus as Savior and Lord will grow deeper. That deepening appreciation will be revealed through his reverence for God and His laws, through a sense of gratitude for all of God's goodness.

(2) **Regarding the meaning of existence**—The Intermediate will grow in his realization that all existence is an expression of God's goodness, wisdom, and power. He will realize that every person, because he is created in the image of God, is of infinite worth, has marvelous possibilities, and possesses spiritual needs that only God can meet.

(3) **Regarding self**—The Intermediate needs to appreciate his body and mind as gifts from God, which should be cared for, developed, and used for God's glory and the good of others. His personal ideal should be the attainment of a mature Christian personality.

(4) **Regarding others**—The young Christian should accept the responsibility for his influence upon others, should develop an attitude of unselfish devotion to the welfare of people of all cultures, races, and social levels, and should feel sincere concern for the salvation of others.

(5) **Regarding divine institutions**—Teachers should help their pupils recognize that the Lord's Day, the ordinances of baptism and the Lord's Supper, and the institution of marriage and family life should be used to honor Christ. They need also to respect civil government and to assume the responsibilities of good citizenship.[16]

If the teacher helps students to grow in these areas, then all of the questions and concerns raised above can be put in proper biblical focus, and the teenagers can receive sound biblical help for coping with their pressures and problems in growing during these critical years.

They can, therefore, develop a Christian philosophy of life. They can be armed and fortified with the Word of God that reminds them that

(1) they are somebody: They are created in the image of God, and have received God's Holy Spirit in conversion, who dwells in them and guides them in all ways of truth. (*John 16:13*)

(2) the cultivating of the Spirit is the most important aspect of growing, and that spiritual things must always be placed before material things. (*Matthew 6:33*)

(3) true happiness comes through trusting and obeying Christ. (*Proverbs 3:5*)

(4) when we trust and obey Christ, God will supply us with every need for every occasion. (*Philippians 4:19*)

(5) Christ will help guide our goals and careers and give us fulfillment in them, because we are following Him. (*Proverbs 3:6*)

(6) we will grow and mature until "we all come in the unity of the faith, and of the knowledge of the Son of God, unto a perfect [mature] man, unto the measure of the stature of the fullness of Christ..." (*Ephesians 4:13-14*, emphasis mine, KJV).

METHODOLOGY

What is the best method to use in order to teach young and older teens? As was pointed out in an earlier chapter and this chapter, there are many methods that one can use when teaching. However, some methods are better adapted to certain age groups. When teaching teens, one can use several methods that are effective. They are as follows:

(1) Assignment   (8) Group discussion

(2) Buzz Session   (9) Field Trips

(3) Debate   (10) Listening

(4) Panel Discussion   (11) Problem Solving

(5) Question   (12) Drama

(6) Review   (13) Music

(7) Project   (14) Role-playing

Of all these methods, I am partial to the assignment/discussion (although I know that any of these methods may be utilized as long as they accomplish the aim of the lesson). I favor this method for teens because the aim in any teaching situation is to make the pupil think and participate to the degree that he or she internalizes the central lesson thought and applies it daily. Good discussion can accomplish this goal because it involves these six steps:

(1) Objectives and aims are clarified;

(2) Problems are analyzed;

(3) Facts are assembled and studied;

(4) Pros and cons are considered;

(5) Advantages and disadvantages are discussed; and,

(6) Efforts are made to arrive at a conclusion.

In the assignment/discussion method, teens can be led to think, participate, internalize, and apply the truths of the Bible. When teachers facilitate this process for teenagers, they are teaching successfully.

NOTES

1. Dorothy Jean Furnish, *Experiencing the Bible with Children* (Nashville: Abington Press, 1991), 38-43.

2. Ibid., 39.

3. Ibid., 40.

4. Ibid., 42-43.

5. Robert Barron, J. Omar Brubaker, Robert E. Clark, *Understanding People: Children, Youth, Adults* (Wheaton: Evangelical Training Association, 1989), 29.

6. Phyllis Heusser, *Understanding and Relating to Children* (Valley Forge: Judson Press, 1983), 10.

7. *Understanding People: Children, Youth, Adults,* 27-28.

8. Phyllis Heusser, 10-11.

9. Ibid., 11.

10. *Understanding People: Children, Youth, Adults,* 35.

11. Phyllis Heusser, 12.

12. Ibid.

13. Ibid., 13.

14. Ibid., 13-14.

15. Annie Ward Byrd, *Better Bible Teaching for Intermediates* (Nashville, Tennessee: The Convention Press, 1959), 26.

16. Ibid., 7.

Chapter VII

The Teacher as Evangelist

All Sunday school and church Bible teachers should concentrate on at least two areas with their students—they must seek to evangelize and nurture. This is especially true for the age groups between the primaries and young people.

Evangelize

What are the prerequisites needed before a church teacher can become a good evangelist? First, the teacher must be born-again—born of the Spirit of God (John 3:3). No teacher can have a strong burden and a strong compassion for the unsaved, unless the fire of the Holy Spirit stirs him or her. Teachers who are truly born-again will look for every opportunity in their classes to witness to an unsaved pupil. The born-again teacher takes seriously Christ's mandate in Acts 1:8: "But you shall receive power when the Holy Spirit has come upon you; and you shall be my witnesses in Jerusalem and in all Judea and Samaria and to the end of the earth" (RSV). Someone has remarked that "If you are going to sell, you must first tell." Teachers must be on fire to tell their story to someone else. They must share it in the classroom as well as outside of the classroom.

Acts 1:8 speaks about sharing the Gospel in Jerusalem, Judea, Samaria, and to the uttermost part of the world. Where is the teacher's Jerusalem? It is her classroom. That is why teachers must know their students individually, especially those between the primary and youth age divisions. Where is the teacher's Jerusalem? It is not only in the classroom; it is also in the home. Is everyone in your home a follower of Jesus Christ? Are all of your sisters and brothers, cousins and relatives saved? Are all of your neighbors committed to Christ? Is everyone on your street a born-again person? This is your Jerusalem where you can "tell" and "sell" the Gospel of Jesus Christ.

Sunday school and Bible class teachers must be as, or more, excited about their product than persons who sell Avon, Amway, and Mary Kay.

Dr. George McCalep, who pastors the Greenforest Baptist Church in Decatur, Georgia—one of the fastest-growing churches in that area—said that he teaches his members to recruit people for Sunday school (and potentially for Christian discipleship) in supermarkets, department stores, at car washes, or anywhere they can be found. Dr. McCalep believes, like many others, that the Sunday school is the best place for doing serious evangelism. Barnette asserts that "The members of the Sunday school and their families constitute the church's greatest evangelistic field."[1] Moreover, he[2] gives five reasons why the Sunday school should be used as the chief evangelistic agency in the church:

(1) The Sunday school has the Bible as the textbook. He states that the Bible is truth and truth is power. Thus, the Sunday school has power to lead sinners to Christ;

(2) The Sunday school has soul winners in its organization. He believes that the Sunday school officers and teachers should make the best and most effective soul winners in a church;

(3) The Sunday school has "the lost" in its membership. As National Baptists, we have not enrolled as many unsaved persons as we could have. In Southern Baptist churches, several hundred thousand unsaved people have been enrolled in Sunday school, and many of them have been later led to Christ and made whole, and have become members of the church.

(4) The Sunday school has the combined influence of the workers. The pastor, superintendent, officers, and teachers, Barnette feels, should combine to make a positive impact on reaching the unsaved.

(5) The Sunday school prepares the hearts of people for the acceptance of the Gospel. Not only does the Sunday school help to prepare the unsaved for the acceptance of the Gospel, but it also prepares the saved for the acceptance of the Gospel. It is easier to preach to a Bible-trained church than it is to preach to a Bible-illiterate congregation.

In our congregation, we believe that Sunday school teachers and workers can be effective soul winners. Therefore, we have recruited many of them and some others have volunteered to become members of weekly witnessing teams. These go witnessing each week and seek to lead the lost to Christ Jesus and His way of life.

In order for the superintendent, teachers, and other Sunday school workers to be effective witnesses for our Lord, they need to be trained in the methods and content of evangelism. On many occasions in our church, the minister of discipleship/evangelism and/or pastor have led in evangelistic workshops in which we teach both the content and methods of evangelizing. We have often had role-playing sessions to allow potential soul winners (witnesses for Christ) to get a feel for what it is like to actually seek to lead an unsaved person to Christ. A few years ago, I wrote some notes for evangelists to use in order to become effective "soul winners." I entitled these notes, "Let's Go Witnessing," and they are presented in the section which follows:

LET'S GO WITNESSING

I. Jesus Christ commanded that all Christians should be His witnesses at home and abroad. "But ye shall receive power, after that the Holy Ghost is come upon you: and ye shall be witnesses unto me both in Jerusalem, and in all Judaea, and in Samaria, and unto the uttermost parts of the earth" (Acts 1:8, KJV).

II. Every church that is serious about obeying Jesus' command will develop teams in the congregation who will systematically witness for our Lord from house to house, in public, and at home.

"And [I] have taught you publickly, and from house to house." (Acts 20:20)

III. The needs of a Christian witness are as follows:
   A. He or she must be a committed Christian; he or she must be born again (John 3:3).
   B. A Christian witness needs to have a burden (concern) for the unsaved and un-churched.
   C. A Christian witness needs to know the plan of salvation:
      1. That everyone needs to be saved from sin because we all have sinned. "For all have sinned, and come short of the glory of God." (Romans 3:23, KJV)
      2. That Jesus Christ is God's solution to the sin problem. "For God so loved the world, that he gave his only begotten Son, that whosoever believeth in him should not perish, but have everlasting life." (John 3:16, KJV)
      3. That whosoever puts his trust in Jesus Christ will be saved. "He that believeth and is baptized shall be saved; but he that believeth not shall be damned." (Mark 16:16, KJV)

         "For by grace are ye saved through faith; and that not of yourselves: it is the gift of God: Not of works, lest any man should boast." (Ephesians 2:8-9, KJV)

         "For whosoever shall call upon the name of the Lord shall be saved." (Romans 10:13, KJV)

         "For the wages of sin is death; but the gift of God is eternal life through Jesus Christ our Lord." (Romans 6:23, KJV)

      4. That the Holy Spirit is given to a person the moment he believes (puts his faith) in Jesus as Savior and Lord. "Then Peter said unto them, Repent, and be baptized every one of you in the name of Jesus Christ for the remission of sins, and ye shall receive the gift of the Holy Ghost." (Acts 2:38, KJV)

         "That which is born of the flesh is flesh; and that which is born of the Spirit is spirit." (John 3:6, KJV)

"In whom ye also trusted, after that ye heard the word of truth, the gospel of your salvation: in whom also after that ye believed, ye were sealed with that holy Spirit of promise." (Ephesians 1:13, KJV)

5. That a Christian is secure in his or her salvation relationship in Jesus Christ. "For whatsoever is born of God overcometh the world: and this is the victory that overcometh the world, even our faith. Who is he that overcometh the world, but he that believeth that Jesus is the Son of God?" (1 John 5:4-5, KJV)

"My sheep hear my voice, and I know them, and they follow me: And I give unto them eternal life; and they shall never perish, neither shall any man pluck them out of my hand. My Father, which gave them me, is greater than all; and no man is able to pluck them out of my Father's hand. I and my Father are one." (John 10:27-30, KJV)

"For whom He foreknew, He also predestined to be conformed to the image of His Son, that He might be the firstborn among many brethren. Moreover whom He predestined, these He also called; whom He called, these He also justified; and whom He justified, these He also glorified." (Romans 8:29-30, NKJV)

"There is therefore now no condemnation to those who are in Christ Jesus, who do not walk according to the flesh, but according to the Spirit." (Romans 8:1, NKJV)

HINTS FOR SUCCESSFUL WITNESSING

1. Set a definite time during the week to go witnessing.
2. Go with another person. Jesus sent out His seventy (70) disciples two by two. (Luke 10:1ff)
3. We should be clean and neat in appearance.
4. Pray before going. Be sure you know the plan of salvation.

5. When going out with someone else, decide which person will lead in the witnessing session. One person should do most of the talking at each setting.
6. Be courteous and polite at all times, even if you are insulted.
7. Stay on the subject. Even if the unsaved or un-churched person tries to get you off the subject, find an effective way to get back on the subject at hand—that is, receiving Jesus Christ as his Savior.
8. After you have thoroughly explained to him the plan of salvation, then ask the person if he or she is ready to receive Jesus as his Savior and Lord. Before leaving, pray for and with him or her. Also, invite him or her to join you in church the following Sunday. Try to sit with him or her.
9. Continue to cultivate a deep concern for the lost and un-churched.
10. Never! Never! Never forget that the primary purpose of the church is to lead other people to Christ—to witness with your words and deeds.

As I write this chapter, we are in the midst of our Vacation Bible School session. It dawns on me that here is another prime opportunity for the Sunday school teachers, Bible teachers, and all who teach during Vacation Bible School to do some serious evangelistic work. There are many unsaved boys and girls who come to Vacation Bible School, but who do not attend Sunday school. This is a good time to sow the seed of the Gospel of Jesus Christ and allow the Holy Spirit to do His work in the hearts of unsaved children.

Also, revivals are good times to do serious evangelistic ministry. Perhaps they are not as popular as they once were, but they are still useful in leading unsaved persons to Jesus Christ. Teachers should lead in the ministry of inviting people to receive Christ during services of revivals and weeks of spiritual renewal. If those who teach the Word of God are not zealous for lost persons, then something is wrong with their commitment to live what they teach. Our church has happily discovered that the prisons are ripe places to lead persons to Christ. Our Jail Ministry Teams have reported more than five baptisms in the last two months. And several of the people on our Jail Ministry Teams are also teachers in our church.

Nurture

I spoke to some extent about this issue in chapter 1. But further discussion needs to be focused on here. In the Great Commission—the Divine Imperative according to Emil Brunner—is the pivotal Scripture for nurturing students in the church setting. Matthew declared that Jesus commanded the church to go forth "and make disciples of all nations, baptizing them in the name of the Father and of the Son and of the Holy Spirit, teaching them to observe all that I (Jesus) have commanded you; and lo, I am with you always, to the close of the age" (Matthew 28:19-20, RSV).

This passage is the church's theological marching orders for making and nurturing disciples. And what better place is there to evangelize and nurture disciples than in the Sunday school and in weekly Bible classes? Once a person has been won to Jesus Christ, then he needs constant training and nurturing. I spoke in another setting about how the church must train to retain. I am thoroughly convinced that if the church is to retain persons, they must be trained. There is no substitute for Christian training and nurturing. This is true because Jesus said so. He declared that the church should teach the new converts "all that" He has commanded them to be taught. That means that the Sunday school and Bible teacher must be deeply rooted in Bible doctrine and Bible principles so that he or she may teach the pupils all that Christ commanded.

Many churches fail at the nurturing level because they are not good Christian fishermen. Once the fish is caught, he must not be left on the bank to rot. Rather, wise fishermen bring the fish home, clean and dress it, and enjoy a good fish meal. The wise teacher leads a student to Christ and then continues to feed that student the

Word of God so that the student can grow and mature to a fuller Christian stature. The reason so many people in churches are tossed to and fro by every wind of doctrine is because they have not been systematically nurtured in the Christian faith. They have not become rooted, grounded, wrapped, and tied into the Word of God. Jesus commanded Peter three times to feed (nurture) His sheep (John 21:15-17).

The early church in the New Testament was a nurturing body of believers. They were serious about teaching the Christian faith in order to build up the body of the church. In Acts 2:41-42 (KJV) we read, "Then they that gladly received his word were baptized: and the same day there were added unto them (the church) about three thousand souls. And they continued stedfastly in the apostles' doctrine and fellowship, and in breaking of bread, and in prayers." We observe again how serious they were in teaching the doctrines of the church to all new converts. Notice the text says that all three thousand persons who were saved and baptized on the Day of Pentecost continued without stopping in their study of the doctrines which the apostles taught them. That is serious nurturing. Our churches today would be much stronger, more stable, more productive, and more mission- and stewardship-oriented if they were taught better the Word of God. (For a more in-depth discussion of this nurturing thrust, see chapter 1.)

In our own church, we have developed a New Members' Orientation class in which all new members are oriented to the life and ministry of our church, and especially are given a fourteen-week study in Baptist doctrine. Many blessings in nurturing have come out of this class. A few persons, at first, slightly resisted the idea. But, by far, the majority has been blessed. My wife, who joined our church a week after our marriage, was a bit hesitant about taking a New Members' Orientation class because she had taught Sunday school in her home church for more than seven years. But after she finished the fourteen-week training sessions in the New Members' Orientation class, she is now one of its biggest advocates. In fact, most of our Sunday school classes in the last eight years have come out of our New Members' Orientation class. (We currently average about five hundred persons each Sunday in Sunday school.) The nurturing and training ministry of our church has blessed all aspects of our church's life and ministry. Without sound teaching, we would not be supporting home and foreign mission as we are. Without sound nurturing and training, we would not have given $110,000 to American Baptist College toward its Chair of Excellence in 1992. Without strong teaching and nurturing, we, currently, would not be building a house for the needy in partnership with Habitat for Humanity. Without sound teaching and nurturing, we would not be involved in a Child Development Center and Academy, which is training our children academically, mentally, socially, morally, and spiritually. Without a strong teaching and nurturing ministry, we would not have grown in our church budget from $72,000 in 1977 to $900,000 in 1992, not including our Child Development Center and Academy budget. We praise God that through sound teaching and nurturing, He has blessed our local congregation in tremendous ways.

Summary

We have indicated that there are two main areas on which the serious teacher/evangelist should concentrate: (1) evangelism and (2) nurture. These are not two separate components, but are two parts of the whole. No teacher can be serious about evangelism without being serious about nurturing disciples. And no teacher can be serious about nurturing disciples without helping them become evangelists along with him or her. Sheep beget sheep. Christians always seek to allow the Spirit to help them reproduce others in Christ.

NOTES

1. J. N. Barnette, *The Place of the Sunday School in Evangelism* (Nashville, Tennessee: Convention Press, 1963), 23.

2. Ibid., 27-32.

Bibliography

Barnette, J. N. *The Place of the Sunday School in Evangelism.* Nashville, Tennessee: Convention Press, 1962.

Barron, Robert, Omar J. Brubaker, and Robert E. Clark. *Understanding People: Children, Youth, Adults.* Wheaton: Evangelical Training Association, 1989.

Binkley, Olin T. *How to Study the Bible.* Nashville, Tennessee: Convention Press, 1969.

Blair, Edward P. *The Bible and You.* Nashville, Tennessee: Abingdon Press, 1953.

Brooks, D. P. *The Bible–How to Understand and Teach It.* Nashville, Tennessee: Broadman Press, 1969.

Charpentier, Etienne. *How to Read the Bible.* New York: Gramercy Publishing Company, 1991.

Colson, Howard P. *Preparing to Teach the Bible.* Nashville, Tennessee: Convention Press, 1959.

Everett, D. Leon, II. *In the Christian Teacher's Workshop.* Nashville, Tennessee: National Baptist Publishing Board, 1986.

Furnish, Dorothy Jean. *Experiencing the Bible with Children.* Nashville, Tennessee: Abingdon Press, 1991.

Hyatt, J. Philip. *The Heritage of Biblical Faith.* Saint Louis, Missouri: The Bethany Press, 1964.

LaHaye, Tim. *How to Study the Bible for Yourself.* Eugene, Oregon: Harvest House Publishers, 1976.

Leavitt, Guy P. *Teach with Success.* Cincinnati, Ohio: Standard Publishing (Revised edition), 1989.

Rusbuldt, Richard E. *Basic Teacher Skills.* Valley Forge, Pennsylvania: Judson Press, 1985.

Sproul, R. C. *Knowing Scripture*. Downers Grove, Illinois: Intervarsity Press, 1977.

Turnbull, Ralph G., ed. *Baker's Dictionary of Practical Theology*. Grand Rapids, Michigan: Baker Book House, 1967.

Weatherspoon, J. B. *The Book We Teach*. Nashville, Tennessee: Convention Press, 1934.

Yates, Kyle M. *Preaching from the Prophets*. Nashville, Tennessee: Broadman Press, 1942.

Pamphlets

Heusser, Phyllis. *Understanding and Relating to Children*, Workshop #11, Vision for Leadership: Resources for Leader Development in a Church. Valley Forge: Judson Press, 1983.

O'Brien, David. *Understanding and Relating to Youth*, Workshop #12, Vision for Leadership: Resources for Leader Development in a Church. Valley Forge: Judson Press, 1983.

Article

Keylock, Leslie R. "Bible Translations: A Guide Through the Forest," in *Christianity Today*, Volume 27 (April, 1983).

NOTES

NOTES

www.ingramcontent.com/pod-product-compliance
Lightning Source LLC
Chambersburg PA
CBHW070953290426
44102CB00008B/125